Praying *with* St. Augustine

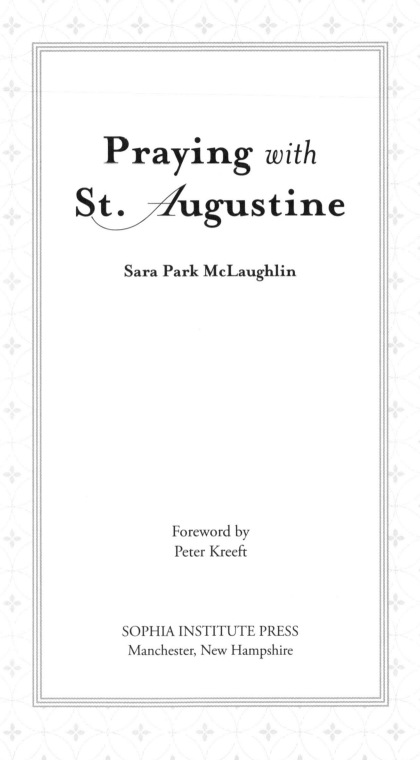

Praying *with* St. Augustine

Sara Park McLaughlin

Foreword by
Peter Kreeft

SOPHIA INSTITUTE PRESS
Manchester, New Hampshire

Cover by Isabella Fasciano

Cover image: St. Augustinus by Antonello da Messina.
Background (Alamy BJFDEM)

Sermon 206, no. 3; *Sermon 123*, no. 5; *Sermon 216*, no. 7; *Sermon 265*, no. 10; *The Free Choice of the Will* 2.16.43; *Sermon 188*, no. 2; *Sermon 184*, no. 3; *Sermon 203*, no. 3; *Sermon 262*, no. 4; *Sermon 262*, nos. 5–6; *Sermon 196*, no. 3; *Sermon 261*, no. 1; *Sermon 261*, no. 9; *The Christian Combat* 11; *Sermon 333*, no. 7; *Sermon 211*, no. 5; *Sermon 132*, no. 4; *Sermon 225*, no. 4; *Sermon 67*, no. 10; and parts of *Confessions* 4.10.15. Translated by Laura Bement. March 2023.

Scripture quotations are taken from the Douay-Rheims edition of the Old and New Testaments.

Sophia Institute Press
Box 5284, Manchester, NH 03108
1-800-888-9344

www.SophiaInstitute.com

Sophia Institute Press® is a registered trademark of Sophia Institute.

paperback ISBN 978-1-64413-864-9

ebook ISBN 978-1-64413-865-6

Library of Congress Control Number: 2023934827

Contents

Praying *with* St. Augustine

Acknowledgments

My sincere thanks to everyone at Sophia Institute Press who helped produce and market this book, especially to Michael Warren Davis, editor, for kindly accepting the manuscript for publication, and to Anna Maria Dube, managing and development editor, for efficiently facilitating the entire process. I also extend my deepest gratitude to Laura Bement, copy editor extraordinaire, whose contributions included not only keen insight and editing but also research and skills as a translator.

I am indebted to Peter Kreeft, PhD, for his encouragement and for graciously writing the foreword.

Ultimately, thanks be to God. *Non nobis Domine, sed Nomini Tuo da gloriam!*—Not to us, Lord, but to Your Name give the glory!

Foreword

IT IS WORTH learning Latin just to read St. Augustine. No Christian writer, perhaps no writer at all, has ever been as eloquent. Few have been as philosophically and theologically profound, or as passionately in love with God (which is the essence of being a saint). Eloquent writers are usually unphilosophical or unsaintly or both (Nietzsche and Oscar Wilde come to mind). Profound philosophers and theologians, even when saintly, are not eloquent (St. Thomas Aquinas), and when eloquent, are not saintly (Plato). The beautiful (eloquence), the true (philosophical wisdom), and the good (sanctity) have never been more completely combined in one writer than in Augustine. Christ, Socrates, and Buddha all wrote nothing.

No passages in Augustine's writings are more eloquent than his prayers, or more profound than his prayers, or more saintly than his prayers, for prayer is the very life-blood of sanctity.

It is therefore inexcusable and scandalous that there are no collections of Augustine's prayers in print. Sara McLaughlin has happily remedied this inexcusable scandal. Her judicious choices show a deep love and appreciation for Augustine as well as a scholar's understanding.

This book is powerful. Anyone who prays these prayers from the heart will be changed from the heart. There should be a warning label attached to this book: "Use of these prayers, especially in a personal way, without the safety net of scholarly distance, may well result in unforeseen consequences. The publisher is not responsible for these consequences. God is." These prayers let God do things to you, in you, with you. To call them expressions of "man's search for God" is, in C. S. Lewis's felicitous words, "like speaking of the mouse's search for the cat."

Lovers often improvise, but lovers also often sing the most beautiful and passionate love songs ever written by others, thus making them their own. I dare you to sing these love songs to the "Hound of Heaven," whose longing for intimate union with you is even more passionate than your longing for intimate union with Him who is infinite beauty, truth, and goodness. That union, after all, is the ultimate end of prayer, and of your whole existence.

— *Peter Kreeft*

Preface

WHAT BETTER WAY could we have to know the heart of a man like St. Augustine than to listen to him pray? As he taught, "Our prayer seeks peace and attains it. For prayer, supported by the distinguished wings of the virtues, flies and is easily borne into Heaven, where Christ, our Peace, has gone before" (*Sermon 206*, no. 3). When we read St. Augustine's vast writings, we discover something of the saint's enormous genius and theological insight. However, through his prayers, we experience his relationship with God.

Evagrius once said, "A theologian is one whose prayer is true." St. Augustine's prayers and his theology are one. All his prayers, even those not explicitly theological, reflect his theology concerning the nature of God, the nature of man, and the proper relationship between God and man. And so, by studying his prayers, we can deepen our understanding of his theology.

I once heard some prayers attributed to St. Augustine at a retreat. Later, I embarked on a quest to purchase a collection of his prayers, but I discovered, upon inquiring at my favorite bookstore, that there was no such book currently on the market. There is no shortage of books about the saint's writings, such as Benedict J. Groeschel's *Augustine: Major Writings* (New York: Crossroad, 1995) and Thomas A. Hand's *Augustine on Prayer* (New York: Catholic Book Publishing Co., 1986), but I found no collection of prayers. This book, therefore, was compiled out of necessity.

Few collections of St. Augustine's prayers have ever existed. Of those I found, none is complete, and the last two are now out of print: *Augustine Day by Day: Minute Meditations for Every Day Taken from the Writings of St. Augustine,* compiled and edited by John E. Rotelle, O.S.A. (New York: Catholic Book Publishing Co., 1986); *The Prayers of St. Augustine,* compiled by Barry Ulanov (Minneapolis: Seabury Press, 1983); and *Praying with St. Augustine,* with an introduction by Murray Watts (New York: Triangle, 1987).

For the purposes of this collection, only those prayers that clearly address God are considered true prayers. I have included as prayers those writings of St. Augustine that quote Scripture and could be characterized as prayers, (i.e., those in which the heart is crying out to God).

To read this book is to become acquainted with some of the most striking, inspirational, beautiful, and often paradoxical prayers ever written. The length of these prayers varies greatly; some prayers are as brief as a few sentences, whereas others, such as some of the prayers from the *Confessions*, extend for more than a page.

The name of the work from which each prayer was taken, as well as the pertinent sermon, book, chapter, and section number, is included in a parenthesis following each prayer. Prayers are grouped thematically, and each section is introduced by a brief overview of the theological doctrines as they are conveyed in the prayers. Most prayers have been lightly edited for consistency in style and language.

Now, as we enter into the words of the holy bishop and saint, let us pray with him in our hearts.

Introduction

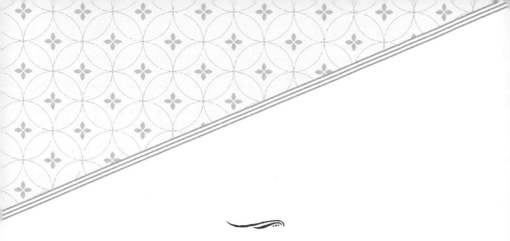

Aurelius Augustinus, who is considered by most to be the greatest Father of the Church, was born on November 13, 354 A.D., in Numidia at Tagaste. The product of a classical education, Augustine spent many formative years espousing the truth of Manichaeism and Neoplatonism as he taught rhetoric in Milan. But in 387, he was baptized by St. Ambrose upon his conversion to Christianity, and in 391, he became a priest.

St. Augustine, who became Bishop of Hippo in 396, is probably most well known for his *Confessions*, the dramatic account of his own conversion, but the prolific writer also left behind more than a hundred works of all kinds, including theological treatises, exegetical writings, sermons, and letters.

St. Augustine's Theology of Prayer
St. Augustine clearly perceived the reciprocal relationship between prayer and faith. He once preached that faith was

the "fountain of prayer.... So then that we may pray, let us believe; and that this same faith whereby we pray fail not, let us pray. Faith pours out prayer, and the pouring out of prayer obtains the strengthening of faith" (*Sermon 65 on the New Testament*, no. 1).

He also believed that prayer sparks our desire for God's answer and readies us to receive His gifts. Recognizing our total dependency on God for all things, even life itself, the saint reminded his listeners in a sermon that "however much you have, no matter how rich you are, you are a beggar of God. This is revealed at the hour of your prayer, and I prove it to you.... For do you not say: 'Give us our daily bread?'" He followed this reminder with an exhortation to give to God what He has given us: "And yet Christ says to you: Give to me from that which I have given to you. For what did you bring when you came here? All the things that you, who were created, have found, I created: you have brought nothing here, and you will take nothing away" (*Sermon 123*, no. 5).

The most comprehensive explanation of St. Augustine's views on prayer are in a letter written to a woman named Proba, a wealthy widow who had asked Augustine what kind of person she should strive to be in order to pray and what things to ask for in prayer. St. Augustine wrote an eloquent discourse on prayer in answer to her questions.

He first writes that we are all pilgrims walking in darkness, and as such, Christian souls on earth ought to feel desolate. Until we attain the true consolation awaiting us in Heaven, we must continue in prayer, walking by faith and not by sight. He warns her against finding false consolation in riches, because they will not last.

Then he addresses the question of how we should pray. Evidently, Proba had been disturbed by the Scripture, "We know not what we should pray for as we ought" (Rom. 8:26). St. Augustine replies that we should pray for a happy or blessed life, because that desire leads us to the Lord, "who is Himself the True Blessed Life" (Letter 130, no. 15).

St. Augustine reminds Proba, and us, that the Lord taught us three valuable lessons about prayer: God "knows what things we have need of before we ask Him," "Men ought always to pray and not to faint," and "Ask, and you shall receive; seek and you shall find; knock, and it shall be opened unto you" (Letter 130, nos. 15–16).

He explains that prayer is not for God's benefit but for ours. It increases our desire and makes us ready to receive His gifts. Furthermore, "when we cherish uninterrupted desire along with the exercise of faith and hope and charity, we 'pray always'" (Letter 130, no. 18). In other words, St. Augustine interprets the Biblical admonition to "pray without ceasing" as "desire without intermission, from

Him who alone can give it, a happy life, which no life can be but that which is eternal" (Letter 130, no. 18). He continues:

> To us, therefore, words are necessary, that by them we may be assisted in considering and observing what we ask, not as means by which we expect that God is to be either informed or moved to compliance. When, therefore, we say, "Hallowed be Thy Name," we admonish ourselves to desire that His name, which is always holy, may be also among men esteemed holy, that is to say, not despised; which is an advantage not to God but to men.
>
> When we say, "Thy Kingdom come," which shall certainly come whether we wish it or not, we do by these words stir up our own desires for that Kingdom, that it may come to us and that we may be found worthy to reign in it.
>
> When we say, "Thy will be done on earth as it is in Heaven," we pray for ourselves that He would give us the grace of obedience, that His will may be done by us in the same way as it is done in heavenly places by angels.
>
> When we say, "Give us this day our daily bread," the words "this day" signify for the present time, in which we ask either for that competency of temporal blessings that I have spoken of before ("bread" being used to designate the whole of those blessings, because of its constituting so important a part of them), or the sacrament of believers, which is in this present time necessary, but necessary in order to obtain the felicity not of the present time but of eternity.
>
> When we say, "Forgive us our debts as we forgive our debtors," we remind ourselves both what we should ask and

what we should do in order that we may be worthy to receive what we ask.

When we say, "Lead us not into temptation," we admonish ourselves to seek that we may not, through being deprived of God's help, be either ensnared to consent or compelled to yield to temptation.

When we say, "Deliver us from evil," we admonish ourselves to consider that we are not yet enjoying that good estate in which we shall experience no evil....

If we pray rightly, and as becomes our wants, we say nothing but what is already contained in the Lord's Prayer. (Letter 130, nos. 21–22)

The letter continues with an insight into the saint's prescription for effective prayer:

Faith, hope, and charity, therefore, lead unto God the man who prays, i.e., who believes, hopes, and desires and is guided as to what he should ask from the Lord by studying The Lord's Prayer. Fasting and abstinence from gratifying carnal desires in other pleasures, without injury to health, and especially frequent almsgiving are a great assistance in prayer; so that we may be able to say, "In the day of my trouble I sought the Lord, with my hands in the night before Him, and I was not deceived." For how can God, who is a Spirit, and who cannot be touched, be sought with hands in any other sense than by good works? (Letter 130, no. 24)

We should keep these words in mind as we read St. Augustine's prayers.

Prayers of Praise

ANYONE WHO HAS read many of the writings of St. Augustine knows that the great saint was a man of praise: "But let my soul praise You so that it may love You; and let it confess Your own mercies to You so that it may praise You" (*Confessions* 5.1.1). Requests were always coupled with sincere praise because he understood the inextricable relationship between prayers of petition and prayers of praise: "Lord, teach me to know and understand which of these should be first: to call on You, or to praise You?" (*Confessions* 1.1.1).

Throughout St. Augustine's sermons and expository writing, thunderous praise to God rings out, but nowhere is praise more evident than in the *Confessions*, his spiritual autobiography. The work even begins on a note of praise: "Great are You, O Lord, and greatly to be praised." And that salutation leads us immediately to the single most well-known passage in all of his works, the key to understanding why praise is the natural, human response to God: "You have made us for Yourself, and our hearts are restless until they rest in You" (*Confessions* 1.1.1).

We praise God because we were made by Him and for Him. And when we become aware that we are in His presence, the only appropriate response is unceasing praise. Alleluia!

1

Great are You, O Lord, and greatly to be praised; great is Your power, and of Your wisdom there is no end. And man, being a part of Your creation, desires to praise You — man, who bears about with him his mortality, the witness of his sin, even the witness that You "resist the proud" — yet man, this part of Your creation, desires to praise You.

You move us to delight in praising You; for You have made us for Yourself, and our hearts are restless until they rest in You.

Lord, teach me to know and understand which of these should be first: to call on You or to praise You; and likewise, to know You or to call on You. But who calls upon You without knowing You? For he that knows You not may call upon You as other than You are.

Or perhaps we call on You so that we may know You. "But how shall they call on Him in whom they have not believed? Or how shall they believe without a preacher?" And those who seek the Lord shall praise Him. For those who seek shall find Him, and those who find Him shall praise Him.

Let me seek You, Lord, in calling on You, and call on You in believing in You; for You have been preached unto us. O Lord, my faith calls on You — that faith which You have imparted to me, which You have breathed into me through the Incarnation of Your Son, through the ministry of Your preacher. (*Confessions* 1.1.1)

2

Hear my prayer, O Lord. Let not my soul faint under Your discipline, nor let me faint in confessing unto You Your mercies, by which You have saved me from all my most mischievous ways, so that You might become sweet to me beyond all the seductions that I used to follow; and so that I may love You entirely and grasp Your hand with my whole heart; and so that You may deliver me from every temptation, even unto the end.

O Lord, my King and my God, for Your service be whatever useful thing I learned as a boy—for Your service what I speak, and write, and count. For when I learned vain things, You granted me Your discipline; and my sin in taking delight in those vanities, You have forgiven me. I learned, indeed, in them many useful words; but these may be learned in things not vain, and that is the safe way for youths to walk in. (*Confessions* 1.15.24)

3

Accept the sacrifice of my confessions by the agency of my tongue, which You have formed and quickened, so that it may confess to Your name. Heal all my bones, and let them say, "Lord, who is like You?" For neither does he who confesses to You teach You what may be passing within him, because a closed heart does not exclude Your eye, nor does man's hardness of heart repulse Your hand, but You dissolve it when You will, either in pity or in vengeance, "and there is no one who can hide himself from Your heart."

But let my soul praise You so that it may love You; and let it confess Your own mercies to You so that it may praise You. Your whole creation ceases not, nor is it silent in Your praises—neither the spirit of man, by the voice directed unto You, nor animal nor corporeal things, by the voice of those meditating thereon; so that our souls may from their weariness arise toward You, leaning on those things that You have made and passing on to You, who has made them wonderfully; and there is there refreshment and true strength. (*Confessions* 5.1.1)

4

For that You are to be praised is shown from the "earth, dragons, and all deeps; fire and hail; snow and vapors; stormy winds fulfilling Your word. Mountains and all hills; fruitful trees and all cedars; beasts and all cattle; creeping things and flying fowl; kings of the earth and all people;

princes and all judges of the earth; both young men and maidens; old men and children" praise Your name.

But when, "from the heavens," these praise You, praise You, our God, "in the heights," all Your "angels," all Your "hosts," "sun and moon," all you stars and light, "the heavens of heavens," and the "waters that be above the heavens," praise Your name, I did not now desire better things, because I was thinking of all; and with a better judgment I reflected that the things above were better than those below, but that all were better than those above alone. (*Confessions* 7.13.19)

5

Let Your works praise You so that we may love You; and let us love You so that Your works may praise You, which have beginning and end from time: rising and setting, growth and decay, form and privation. They have therefore their successions of morning and evening, partly hidden, partly apparent; for they were made from nothing by You, not of You, nor of any matter not Yours, or which was created before, but of concreated matter (that is, matter at the same time created by You), because without any interval of time, You formed its formlessness.

For since the matter of Heaven and earth is one thing, and the form of Heaven and earth another, You have made the matter indeed of almost nothing, but the form of the world You have formed of formless matter; both, however, at the same time, so that the form should follow the matter with no interval of delay. (*Confessions* 13.33.48)

6

O people who are created, praise your God! You who are created, praise your Lord! Because you are nursed, praise Him! Because you are fed, praise Him! Because you are nourished, advance in age and wisdom. (*Sermon 216*, no. 7)

7

We bless the Lord our God, who gathered us together to spiritual joy. Let us be ever in humility of heart, and let our joy be with Him. Let us not be elated with any prosperity of this world, but let us know that our happiness is not until these things shall have passed way.... Let our joy be in hope: let none rejoice as in a present thing, lest he stick fast in the way.

Let joy be wholly of hope to come, desire be wholly of eternal life. Let all sighings breathe after Christ. Let that fairest One alone, who loved the foul to make them fair, be all our desire; after Him alone let us run, for Him alone pant and sigh; "and let them say always, 'The Lord be magnified, that wish the peace of His servant.'" (*Tractates on the Gospel of John* 10.13)

8

The Holy Spirit came. Those whom He first filled spoke in the languages of every nation. When each man spoke every language, what could it mean except for unity in all speech?

Holding on to this idea, confirmed, strengthened, and fastened in this unshaken charity, let us children praise the Lord, and let us say "Alleluia." But in one part? And from where? And to what extent? "From the rising of the sun until its setting, praise the Name of the Lord." (*Sermon 265*, no. 10)

9

"O Lord, truly I am Your servant; I am Your servant, and the son of Your handmaid: You have loosed my bonds. I will offer to You the sacrifice of thanksgiving." Let my heart and my tongue praise You, and let all my bones say, "Lord, who is like You?" Let them so say, and answer me, and "say unto my soul, I am Your salvation." (*Confessions* 9.1.1)

10

"Let every land worship You, and play to You, play to Your name, O Most Highest." A little before, Most Lowly, now Most Highest: Most Lowly in the hands of lying enemies; Most Highest above the heads of praising angels. "Let every land worship You, and play to You, play to Your name, O Most Highest." (*Exposition on Psalm 66*, no. 9)

11

"For better is Your mercy than lives: my lips shall praise You." My lips would not praise You unless Your mercy were to go before me. By Your gift I praise You, through Your mercy I praise You. For I should not be able to praise God unless He gave me the ability to praise Him. "For better is Your mercy than lives: my lips shall praise You." (*Exposition on Psalm 63*, no. 12)

12

"Let my mouth be fulfilled with praise, that with hymn I may tell of Your glory, all the day long Your magnificence." What is "all day long"? Without intermission. In prosperity, because You comfort; in adversity, because You correct: before I was in being, because You made; when I was in being, because You gave health: when I had sinned, because You forgave; when I was converted, because You helped; when I had persevered, because You crowned. So indeed "let my mouth be fulfilled with praise, that with hymn I may tell of Your glory, all the day long Your magnificence." (*Exposition on Psalm 71*, no. 10)

13

O God most high, three persons, but one essence, the same majesty and power, Lord God Almighty! The least of all Your servants, and meanest member of Your mystical Body, the Church, desires to ascribe to You all honor and praise, the utmost that the little knowledge and power with which You have been pleased to endue him is capable of. I have no present but myself to make, and that which is not in itself worthy of Your acceptance, I beg that You will be pleased to look upon, not according to its own value but according to Your own rich mercy, and that sincerity and faith unfeigned, with which I most joyfully consecrate it to Your service.

I believe in and heartily pray to You, great King of Heaven and earth; I acknowledge Father, Son, and Holy Spirit; three Persons, but one essence; the true, the Almighty God, of one compounded, incorporeal, invisible, uncircumscribed Being; in whom there is nothing higher or lower, greater or less, but perfect and equal all: great without quantity, good without quality, eternal without time, life without death, strength without weakness, truth without falsehood, omnipresent without space, filling all things and places without extension, passing everywhere without motion, abiding everywhere without confinement, communicating to all Your creatures without diminishing Your own fullness, governing all things without labor; without beginning, and yet giving beginning to all, making all things mutable, and yet unchangeable Yourself; infinite in greatness, unbounded in power, of goodness indefectible, of wisdom incomprehensible, wonderful in Your counsels, just in Your judgments, unsearchable in Your thoughts, true in all Your words, holy in all Your works, abundant in mercies, longsuffering toward sinners, compassionate to all that repent; always the same, without mixture or defilement, allay or accidents; eternal, immortal, unchangeable.

Your will alters not, Your justice is not biased, Your mind is not disturbed with griefs or pleasures or passions: with You nothing is forgotten, nothing that was once lost called to remembrance again; but all things past or future are ever present to Your capacious mind, whose duration neither begun in time, nor increases by length of time, nor shall it ever end, but You live before, and in, and after all ages. Your glory is eternal, Your power supreme, Your Kingdom everlasting, and world without end. Amen. (*Meditations* 1.12)

14

All honor and praise be to You for His miraculous Incarnation and holy Nativity, whereby He took flesh of
the substance of His Blessed Mother for us and for our
salvation, so that just as He had been before from all
eternity very God of God, so He might be in time very
Man of man.

All honor and thanksgiving be unto You, O Father
forever, for that shedding of His most precious Blood by
which we are redeemed, and for the sweet pledges and
lively memorials of that love, the holy and life-giving sac-
rament of His Body and Blood, by which the members of
Your Church were supplied with daily food from Heaven,
washed and sanctified from their sins, and admitted to be
partakers of the divine nature. (*Meditations* 1.14)

15

Let us magnify that great God, whom angels praise, whom
dominions adore, whom powers fall down and tremble
before; whose excellent glory cherubim and seraphim
proclaim with loud incessant voices: Let us then bear a
part, too, in this heavenly song, and together with angels

and archangels, and with all the company of Heaven, laud and magnify that glorious Name. Let us tune our voices with theirs, and although we cannot reach their pitch, we will exert the utmost of our skill and power in this tribute to the same common Lord and say with them as poor mortals are able, "Holy, holy, holy, Lord God of hosts; Heaven and earth are full of Your glory; glory be to You, O Lord most high!" (*Meditations* 1.26)

Prayers Revealing
God's Attributes

ST. AUGUSTINE BELIEVED that God's nature is reflected in the beauty of creation. Wisdom, Light, Goodness, our Refuge — these and many other of God's attributes are enumerated in these eloquent prayers, such as in this excerpt: "O Eternal Truth, and true Love, and loved Eternity! You are my God; to You do I sigh both night and day" (*Confessions* 7.10.16).

St. Augustine's prayers are fiercely Trinitarian, and they provide a theological discourse or apologetic on the uniquely Christian doctrine of the Trinity: "O Lord our God, we believe in You, the Father and the Son and the Holy Spirit. For the Truth would not say, 'Go, baptize all nations in the name of the Father and of the Son and of the Holy Spirit,' unless You were a Trinity." (*On the Trinity* 15.28.51).

Conveyed in these prayers is an enviable closeness to God, a familiarity that seems to be in keeping with Christ's example to us when he calls the Father "Abba." Intimate yet respectful, the manner with which God is addressed reveals profound awe as well as familial love.

There is also an emphasis on God's nature as paradox, which is seen in references to a God who is merciful yet just; unchangeable yet always changing; never new, never old; still gathering yet lacking nothing.

May St. Augustine's revealed insights into the nature of God illumine our minds and hearts as we read these prayers.

1

O Wisdom! O sweetest Light of the mind made pure! Woe to those who abandon You as leader and wander in Your footsteps, who love Your signs instead of You and who forget what You signify. For You do not cease to signify to us what and how great You are, and every splendor of Creation is a sign of You. (*The Free Choice of the Will* 2.16.43)

2

Let us say then to the Lord our God, "Lord, You have become our refuge from generation to generation." In the first and second generations, You have become our refuge. You were our refuge so that we who before were not might be born.

You were our refuge so that we who were evil might be born anew. You were a refuge to feed those who forsake You.

You are a refuge to raise up and direct Your children. "You have become our refuge." We will not go back from You, for You have delivered us from all our evils and filled us with Your own good things. You give good things now. You deal softly with us so that we may not become wearied in the way. You correct, chastise, smite, and direct us so that we may not wander from the way.

Whether, therefore, You deal softly with us so that we may not become wearied in the way or chastise us so that we may not wander from the way, "You have become our refuge, O Lord." (*Sermon 5 on the New Testament,* no. 6)

3

"Such knowledge is too wonderful for me: it is high, I cannot attain unto it." For I understand by myself how wonderful and incomprehensible is Your knowledge, by which You made me, when I cannot even comprehend myself whom You have made! And yet, "while I was musing, the fire burned," so that "I seek Your face evermore." (*On the Trinity* 15.7.13)

4

O Lord our God, we believe in You: the Father, the Son, and the Holy Spirit. For the Truth would not say, "Go, baptize all nations in the name of the Father and of the Son and of the Holy Spirit," unless You were a Trinity. Nor would you, O Lord God, bid us to be baptized in the name of Him who is not the Lord God. Nor would the divine voice have said, "Hear, O Israel, the Lord your God is one God," unless You were so a Trinity as to be one Lord God.

And if You, O God, were Yourself the Father, and were Yourself the Son, Your Word Jesus Christ, and the Holy Spirit, Your Gift, we should not read in the book of truth,

"God sent His Son"; nor would You, O Only Begotten, say of the Holy Spirit, "whom the Father will send in my name"; and, "whom I will send to you from the Father."

Directing my purpose by this rule of faith, so far as I have been able, so far as You have made me to be able, I have sought You and have desired to see with my understanding what I believed; and I have argued and labored much.

O Lord my God, my one hope, hearken to me, lest through weariness I be unwilling to seek You, "but that I may always ardently seek Your face." O God, You have made me to find You, and You have given the hope of finding You more and more; give me strength to seek.

My strength and my infirmity are in Your sight: preserve the one, and heal the other. My knowledge and my ignorance are in Your sight; where You have opened to me, receive me as I enter; where You have closed, open to me as I knock. May I remember You, understand You, love You. Increase these things in me until You renew me wholly.

I know it is written, "In the multitude of speech, you shall not escape sin." But oh that I might speak only in preaching Your Word and in praising You! Not only should I so flee from sin, but I should earn good desert, however much I so spoke.

For a man blessed of You would not enjoin a sin upon his own true son in the faith, to whom he wrote, "Preach the Word: be instant in season, out of season." Are we to say that he has not spoken much who was not silent about Your Word, O Lord, not only in season but out of season? But therefore it was not much, because it was only what was necessary.

Set me free, O God, from that multitude of speech that I suffer inwardly in my soul, wretched as it is in Your sight, and flying for refuge to Your mercy; for I am not silent in thoughts, even when silent in words.

And if, indeed, I thought of nothing save what pleased You, certainly I would not ask You to set me free from such multitude of speech. But many are my thoughts, such as You know, "thoughts of man, since they are vain."

Grant to me not to consent to them; and if ever they delight me, nevertheless to condemn them and not to dwell in them, as though I slumbered. Nor let them so prevail in me as that anything in my acts should proceed from them; but at least let my opinions, let my conscience, be safe from them, under Your protection.

When the wise man spoke of You in his book, which is now called by the special name of Ecclesiasticus, he said, "We speak much, and yet come short; and in sum of words, He is all." When, therefore, we shall have come to

You, these very many things that we speak, and yet come short, will cease; and You, as One, will remain "all in all." And we shall say one thing without end, in praising You in One, ourselves also made one in You.

O Lord the one God, God the Trinity, whatever I have said in these books that is of Yours, may they who are Yours acknowledge; if anything of my own, may it be pardoned both by You and by those who are Yours. (*On the Trinity* 15.28.51)

5

O God, Founder of the Universe, help me: that, first of all, I may pray aright, and next, that I may act as one worthy to be heard by You: and, finally, set me free.

God, through whom all things are that of themselves could have no being.

God, who does not permit to perish that whose tendency is to destroy itself!

God, who created out of nothing this world, which the eyes of all perceive to be most beautiful!

God, who does not cause evil but does cause that it shall not become the worst!

God, who reveals that evil is nothing to those few fleeing for refuge to that which truly is!

God, through whom the universe, even with its perverse part, is perfect!

God, to whom dissonance is nothing, since in the end the worst resolves into harmony with the better!

God, whom every creature capable of loving loves, whether consciously or unconsciously!

God, in whom all things are, yet whom the shame of no creature in the universe disgraces, nor his malice harms, nor his error misleads!

God, who does not permit any save the pure to know the true!

God, Father of Truth, Father of Wisdom, Father of the True and Perfect Life, Father of Blessedness, Father of the Good and the Beautiful, Father of Intelligible Light, Father of our awakening and enlightening, Father of that pledge that warns us to return to You!

I invoke You, God, Truth, in whom and by whom and through whom are all things true that are true.

God, Wisdom, in whom and by whom and through whom are all wise who are wise.

God, true and perfect Life, in whom and by whom and through whom those live who do truly and perfectly live.

God, Blessedness, in whom and by whom and through whom are all blessed who are blessed.

God, the Good and the Beautiful, in whom and by whom and through whom are all things good and beautiful that are good and beautiful.

God, Intelligible Light, in whom and by whom all shine intelligibly who do intelligibly shine.

God, whose Kingdom is that whole realm unknown to sense.

God, from whose Kingdom law for even these lower realms is derived.

God, from whom to turn is to fall; to whom to turn is to rise; in whom to abide is to stand.

God, from whom to go out is to waste away; unto whom to return is to revive; in whom to dwell is to live.

God, whom no one, unless deceived, loses; whom no one, unless admonished, seeks; whom no one, unless purified, finds.

God, whom to abandon is to perish; whom to long for is to love; whom to see is to possess.

God, to whom faith excites, hope uplifts, love joins.

God, through whom we overcome the enemy, You do I supplicate!

God, whose gift it is that we do not utterly perish.

God, by whom we are warned to watch.

God, through whom we discriminate good things from evil things.

God, through whom we flee from evil and follow after good.

God, through whom we yield not to adversity.

God, through whom we both serve well and rule well.

God, through whom we discern that certain things we had deemed essential to ourselves are truly foreign to us, while those we had deemed foreign to us are essential.

God, through whom we are not held fast by the baits and seductions of the wicked.

God, through whom the decrease of our possessions does not diminish us.

God, through whom our better part is not subject to our worse.

God, through whom death is swallowed up in victory!

God, who turns us about in the way.

God, who strips us of that which is not and clothes us with that which is.

God, who makes us worthy of being heard.

God, who defends us.

God, who leads us into all truth.

God, who speaks all good things to us.

God, who does not deprive us of sanity nor permit another to do so.

God, who recalls us to the path.

God, who leads us to the door.

God, who causes that it is opened to those who knock.

God, who gives us the Bread of Life.

God, through whom we thirst for that water, which having drunk, we shall never thirst again.

God, who convinces the world of sin, of righteousness, and of judgment.

God, through whom the unbelief of others does not move us.

God, through whom we reprobate the error of those who deem that souls have no deserving in Your sight.

God, through whom we are not in bondage to weak and beggarly elements.

God, who purifies and prepares us for divine rewards, propitious, come to me!

In whatever I say, come to my help, O one God, one true Eternal Substance, in whom is no discord, no confusion, no change, no want, no death: in whom is all harmony, all illumination, all steadfastness, all abundance, all life: in whom nothing is lacking and nothing redundant; where Begetter and Begotten are one.

God, whom all things serve that do serve and whom every good soul obeys!

God, by whose laws the poles rotate, the stars pursue their courses, the sun leads on the day, the moon tempers the night, and the whole order of the universe—through days by the alternations of light and darkness; through months by the waxing and waning of moons; through years by the successions of spring, summer, autumn, and winter; through cycles by the completing of the sun's course; through vast eons of time by the return of the stars to their first risings—preserves by these unvarying repetitions of periods, so far as sensible matter may, the marvelous immutability of things.

God, by whose laws forever standing, the unstable motion of mutable things is not allowed to fall into confusion and is, throughout the circling ages, recalled by curb and bit to the semblance of stability; by whose laws the will of the soul is free and rewards to the good, and penalties to the wicked, are everywhere distributed by unchangeable necessity.

God, by whom all good flows toward us, all evil is driven from us.

God, above whom, outside whom, without whom, is nothing.

God, beneath whom, in whom, with whom, is everything; who has made man after Your own image and likeness, which he who knows himself discovers.

Hear, hear, hear me! My God, my Master, my King, my Father, my Cause, my Hope, my Wealth, my Honor, my Home, my Country, my Salvation, my Light, my Life!

Hear, hear, hear me, in that way of Yours known best to few!

At last I love You alone, follow You alone, seek You alone, am I ready to serve You alone: for You alone, by right, are ruler; under Your rule I wish to be.

Command, I pray, and order what You will, but heal and open my ears that I may hear Your commands; heal and open my eyes that I may see Your nod.

Cast all unsoundness from me so that I may recognize You!

Tell me where to direct my gaze so that I may look upon You, and I hope that I shall do all things that You command!

Receive, I pray, Master and most merciful Father, me, Your fugitive! I have suffered already enough punishment, long enough been in bondage to Your enemies whom You have under Your feet, long enough been the sport of delusions. Receive me, Your household servant, fleeing from them, for even these received me, though alien to them, fleeing from You!

I feel that I ought to return to You: let Your door open to me knocking: teach me how to come to You! I have

nothing other than the will: I know nothing other than
that the fleeting and the falling should be spurned, the
fixed and eternal sought after. This I do, Father, for this
is all I know: but how to make my way to You I know
not. Suggest it, make it plain, equip me for the journey!

If they who take refuge in You find You by faith, give
me faith! If by virtue, give me virtue! If by knowledge,
give me knowledge! Increase my faith, increase my hope,
increase my charity, O Goodness unique and admirable!

After You am I groping, and by whatsoever things You
may be felt after, even these do I seek from You! For if
You desert a man, he perishes: but You desert him not,
for You are the sum of good, and no man, seeking You
aright, has failed to find You; and everyone seeks You
aright whom You cause to so seek You.

Cause me, O Father, to seek You; let me not stray
from the path, and let nothing befall me, seeking You, in
place of Yourself! If I desire nothing beside You, let me,
I implore, find You now; but if there is in me the desire
for something beside You, purify me Yourself, and make
me fit to look upon You!

For the rest, whatever concerns the welfare of this
mortal body of mine, so long as I do not know how it
may serve either myself or those I love, to You, Father,

wisest and best, do I commit it, and I pray that You will admonish me concerning it as shall be needful.

But I implore Your most excellent mercy that You convert me in my inmost self to You, and, as I incline toward You, let nothing oppose; and command that so long as I endure and care for this same body, I may be pure and magnanimous and just and prudent, a perfect lover and learner of Your wisdom, a fit inhabitant of a dwelling place in Your most Blessed Kingdom!

Amen and Amen! (*Soliloquies* 1.2–6)

6

And how shall I call upon my God—my God and my Lord? For when I call on Him, I ask Him to come into me. And what place is there in me into which my God can come—into which God can come, even He who made Heaven and earth?

Is there anything in me, O Lord my God, that can contain You? Do indeed Heaven and earth, which You have made, and in which You have made me, contain You? Or, as nothing could exist without You, does whatever exists contain You?

Why, then, do I ask You to come into me, since I indeed exist and could not exist if You were not in me? Because I am not yet in Hell, though You are even there; for "if I go down into Hell, You are there."

I could not, therefore, exist, could not exist at all, O my God, unless You were in me. Or should I not rather say that I could not exist unless I were in You, from whom are all things, by whom are all things, in whom are all things? Even so, Lord; even so. Where do I call You to, since You are in me, or from where can You come into me? For where outside Heaven and earth can I go that from there my God, who has said, "I fill Heaven and earth" may come into me? (*Confessions* 1.2.2)

7

What, then, are You, O my God—what, I ask, but the Lord God? For who is Lord but the Lord? Or who is God save our God? Most high, most excellent, most potent, most omnipotent; most piteous and most just; most hidden and most near; most beauteous and most strong; stable, yet contained of none; unchangeable, yet changing all things; never new, never old; making all things new, yet bringing old age upon the proud, and they know it not; always working, yet ever at rest; gathering, yet needing nothing; sustaining, pervading, and protecting; creating, nourishing, and developing; seeking, and yet possessing all things.

You love, yet You burn not; You are jealous, yet You are free from care; You repent, yet You have no sorrow; You are angry, yet You are serene; You change Your ways, yet You leave Your plans unchanged; You recover what You find, having yet never lost; You are never in want, while You rejoice in gain; You are never covetous, though requiring usury.

That You may owe, more than enough is given to You, yet who has anything that is not Yours? You pay debts while owing nothing; and when You forgive debts, You lose nothing. Yet, O my God, my Life, my holy Joy, what is this that I have said? And what says any man when he speaks of You? Yet woe to those who keep silence, seeing that even they who say most are as the dumb. (*Confessions* 1.4.4)

8

You, O Lord, who lives forever and in whom nothing dies (since before the world was, and indeed before all that can be called "before," You existed, and You are the God and Lord of all Your creatures; and with You fixedly abide the causes of all unstable things, the unchanging sources of all things changeable, and the eternal reasons of all things unreasoning and temporal), tell me, Your suppliant, O God; tell, O merciful One, Your miserable servant—tell me whether my infancy succeeded another age of mine that had at that time perished.

Was it that which I passed in my mother's womb? For of that something has been made known to me, and I have myself seen women with child. And what, O God, my joy, preceded that life? Was I, indeed, anywhere or anybody? For no one can tell me these things, neither father nor mother, nor the experience of others, nor my own memory. Do you laugh at me for asking such things and command me to praise and confess You for what I know?

I give thanks to You, Lord of Heaven and earth, giving praise to You for my first being and infancy, of which I have no memory; for You have granted to man that from others he should come to conclusions about himself, and that he should believe many things concerning himself on the authority of feeble women.

Even then I had life and being; and as my infancy closed, I was already seeking for signs by which my feelings might be made known to others. Where could such a creature come from but from You, O Lord? Or shall any man be skillful enough to fashion himself? Or is there any other vein by which being and life runs into us save this, that "You, O Lord, have made us," with whom being and life are one because You Yourself are Being and Life in the highest?

You are the highest. "You change not," neither in You does this present day come to an end, though it does end in You, since in You all such things are; for they would have no way of passing away unless You sustained them. And since "Your years shall have no end," Your years are an ever present day.

How many of ours and our fathers' days have passed through this Your day and received from it their measure and fashion of being, and others yet to come shall so receive and pass away! "But You are the same"; and all the things of tomorrow and the days yet to come, and all of yesterday and the days that are past, You will do today, You have done today.

What is it to me if any do not understand? Let him still rejoice and say, "What is this?" Let him rejoice even so, and let him rather love to discover in failing to discover than in discovering not to discover You. (*Confessions* 1.6.9–10)

9

Blessed be he who loves You, and his friend in You, and his enemy for Your sake. For he alone loses none dear to him to whom all are dear in Him who cannot be lost.

And who is this but our God, the God that created Heaven and earth and fills them, because by filling them He created them? None loses You but he who leaves You. And he who leaves You, where does he go, or where does he flee to, but from You well pleased to You angry? For where does he not find Your law in his own punishment? "And Your law is the truth," and the truth is You. (*Confessions* 4.9.14)

10

For You will light my candle; the Lord my God will enlighten my darkness; and "of His fullness have all we received," for "that was the true Light that lighted every man that comes into the world"; for in You there is "no variableness, neither shadow of turning." (*Confessions* 4.15.25)

11

O Lord our God, under the shadow of Your wings let us hope. Defend us and carry us. You will carry us when little, and even to grey hairs You will carry us; for our firmness, when it is You, then is it firmness; but when it is our own, then it is infirmity. Our goodness lives always with You, from which when we are averted, we are perverted.

Let us now, O Lord, return so that we be not over-turned, because with You our goodness lives without any eclipse, which goodness You are Yourself. And we need not fear lest we should find no place unto which to return because we fell away from it; for when we were absent, our home — Your Eternity — fell not. (*Confessions* 4.16.31)

12

Does, then, O Lord God of truth, whosoever knows those things therefore please You? For unhappy is the man who knows all those things but knows You not; but happy is he who knows You, though these things he may not know. But he who knows both You and them is not the happier on account of them but is happy on account of You only, if knowing You he glorifies You as God, and gives thanks, and becomes not vain in his thoughts.

A man who knows how to possess a tree and renders thanks to You for its use, even though he may not know how high it is or how wide it spreads, is happier than he who measures it and counts all its branches yet neither owns it nor knows or loves its Creator. The same is true of the just man, whose is the entire world of wealth and who has nothing yet possesses all things by cleaving unto You, to whom all things are subservient, although he does not know even the stars of the Great Bear,[1] yet it is foolish to doubt that this just man is better than one who can measure the heavens, number the stars, and weigh the elements but is forgetful of You, who has set in order all things in number, weight, and measure. (*Confessions* 5.4.7)

---

[1] Known to modern readers as the "Big Dipper." The "Big Dipper" is part of the constellation of Ursa Major, which in Latin means Great Bear.

13

O Eternal Truth, and true Love, and beloved Eternity! You are my God; to You do I sigh both night and day.

When I first knew You, You lifted me up so that I might see there was that which I might see, and that yet it was not I that did see. And You beat back the infirmity of my sight, pouring forth upon me most strongly Your beams of light, and I trembled with love and fear; and I found myself to be far off from You, in the region of dissimilarity, as if I heard this voice of Yours from on high: "I am the food of strong men; grow, and you shall feed upon Me; nor shall you convert Me, like the food of your flesh, into you, but you shall be converted into Me."

And I learned that You correct man for iniquity, and You make my soul consume away like a spider. And I said, "Is Truth, therefore, nothing because it is neither diffused through space, finite, nor infinite?" And You cried to me from afar, "Yea, verily, 'I Am that I Am.'"

And I heard this, as things are heard in the heart, nor was there room for doubt; and I should more readily doubt that I live than that Truth is not, which is "clearly seen, being understood by the things that are made." (*Confessions* 7.10.16)

14

Too late did I love You, O Fairness, so ancient, and yet so new! Too late did I love You!

For behold, You were within, and I without, and there did I seek You; I, unlovely, rushed heedlessly among the things of beauty You made. You were with me, but I was not with You. Those things kept me far from You, which, unless they were in You, were not.

You called and cried aloud and forced open my deafness. You gleamed and shined and chased away my blindness. You exhaled sweet perfumes, and I drew in my breath and panted after You. I tasted and hungered and thirst. You touched me, and I burned for Your peace. (*Confessions* 10.27.38)

15

O Lord my God, what is that secret place of Your mystery, and how far from there have the consequences of my transgressions cast me?

Heal my eyes so that I may enjoy Your light. Surely, if there be a mind so greatly abounding in knowledge and foreknowledge to which all things past and future are so known as one psalm is well known to me, that mind is exceedingly wonderful and very astonishing; because whatever is so past, and whatever is to come of after ages, is no more concealed from Him than was it hidden from me when singing that psalm, what and how much of it had been sung from the beginning, what and how much remained unto the end.

But far be it that You, the Creator of the universe, the Creator of souls and bodies, far be it that You should know all things future and past. Far, far more wonderfully, and far more mysteriously, You know them. For it is not as the feelings of one singing known things or hearing a known song—through expectation of future words and in remembrance of those that are past—are varied, and his senses divided, that anything happens unto You, unchangeably eternal, that is, the truly eternal Creator of minds.

As, then, You in the Beginning knew Heaven and the earth without any change of Your knowledge, so in the Beginning You made Heaven and earth without any distraction of Your action. Let him who understands confess unto You; and let him who understands not confess unto You. Oh, how exalted are You, and yet the humble in heart are Your dwelling place; for You raise up those that are bowed down, and they whose exaltation You are fall not. (*Confessions* 11.31.41)

16

You, therefore, O Lord, who are not one thing in one place and otherwise in another but the Self-same, and the Self-same, and the Self-same, Holy, Holy, Holy, Lord God Almighty, did in the beginning, which is of You, in Your Wisdom, which was born of Your Substance, create something, and that out of nothing.

For You created Heaven and earth not out of Yourself, for then they would be equal to Your Only Begotten and thereby even to You; and in no wisdom would it be right that anything should be equal to You that was not of You.

And there was not anything else except You from which You might create these things, O God, One Trinity and Trine Unity; and, therefore, out of nothing You created Heaven and earth — a great thing and a small, because You are Almighty and Good, to make all things good, even the great Heaven and the small earth.

You were, and there was nought else from which You created Heaven and earth: two such things, one near unto You, the other near to nothing — one to which You should be superior, the other to which nothing should be inferior. (*Confessions* 12.7.7)

17

Behold: now the Trinity appears unto me in an enigma, which You, O my God, are, since You, O Father, in the Beginning of our wisdom—which is Your Wisdom, born of Yourself, equal and coeternal unto You—that is, in Your Son, have created Heaven and earth. ...

And under the name of God, I now held the Father, who made these things; and under the name of the Beginning, the Son, in whom He made these things; and believing, as I did, that my God was the Trinity, I sought further in His holy words, and behold, Your Spirit was borne over the waters. Behold the Trinity, my God, Father, Son, and Holy Spirit—the Creator of all creation. (*Confessions* 13.5.6)

18

My Father, supremely good, beauty of all things beautiful. O Truth, Truth! How inwardly even then did the marrow of my soul pant after You, when they frequently, and in a multiplicity of ways, and in numerous and huge books, sounded out Your name to me, though it was but a voice!

And these were the dishes in which they served to me, hungering for You, the sun and moon instead of You: Your beauteous works but yet Your works, not Yourself, nor Your first works. For before these corporeal works are Your spiritual ones, celestial and shining though they be.

But I hungered and thirsted not even after those first works of Yours but after You Yourself, the Truth, "with whom is no variableness, neither shadow of turning." (*Confessions* 3.6.10)

19

"Turn us again, O Lord God of Hosts, cause Your face to shine; and we shall be saved." For wherever the soul of man turns itself, unless toward You, it is affixed to sorrows, although it is affixed to beauteous things without You and without itself.

And yet these things were not unless they were from You. They rise and set; and by rising, they begin, as it were, to be; and they grow so that they may become perfect; and when they are perfect, they wax old and perish; and while not all wax old, all perish.

Therefore, when things rise and emerge into being, as rapidly as they grow into being, so much more do they hasten into non-being. This is the way of them. You have given them so much, because they are parts of things that do not all exist at the same time; but by departing and succeeding, they together make up the universe, of which they are parts.

And even thus is our speech accomplished by signs emitting a sound; but this, again, is not perfected unless one word pass away when it has sounded its part, in order that another may succeed it.

Let my soul praise You out of all these things, O God, the Creator of all; but let not my soul be fixed on these things by a bond of affection, through the senses of the body. For these things go where they were to go, that they might no longer be; and they rend my soul with pestilent desires, because she longs to be and yet loves to rest in what she loves.

But in these things no place is to be found; they stay not — they flee; and who is he that is able to follow them with the senses of the flesh? Or who can grasp them, even when they are near?

For tardy is the sense of the flesh, because it is the sense of the flesh, and its boundary is itself. It suffices for that for which it was made, but it is not sufficient to hold things running their course from their appointed starting place to the end appointed. For in Your Word, by which they were created, they hear the *fiat*, "Hence and hitherto." (*Confessions* 4.10.15)

20

"You, O Lord, have stretched forth Your hand over the wrath of my enemies"; over that which my enemies can do, You have stretched forth Your hand. For my enemies cannot separate me from You: but You avenge me the more, the more You delay; "over the wrath of my enemies, You have stretched forth Your hand."

Let my enemy rage as he will. He cannot separate me from God: but You, O God, do not yet receive me, weary me in my wanderings, do not give me Your joy and sweetness, have not "inebriated me with the plenteousness of Your house," have not "given me to drink of the torrent of Your pleasure. For with You is the well of life; in Your light we shall see light."

But, oh! I have given You the firstfruits of my spirit, and have believed in You, and "with my mind I serve the law of God": yet still "we ourselves groan within ourselves, waiting for the adoption, the redemption of our bodies."

... "You have stretched forth Your hand over the wrath of my enemies": yet not to make me despair; for it follows, "and Your right hand has made me safe." (*Exposition on Psalm 138*, no. 13)

21

"O Lord, my Helper, and my Redeemer." O Lord, my Helper, in my approach to You! For You are my Redeemer so that I might set out to You, lest any, attributing his conversion to You to his own wisdom, or his attaining You to his own strength, should be rather driven back by You, who resist the proud; for he is not cleansed from the great offense nor pleasing in Your sight. You redeem us so that we may be converted, and You help us so that we may attain You. (*First Exposition on Psalm 19*, no. 15)

22

"O Lord, my Helper and my Redeemer." Helper in good, Redeemer from evil. Helper, that I may dwell in Your love; Redeemer, that You may deliver me from my iniquity. (*Second Exposition on Psalm 19*, no. 16)

23

"For You will light my candle, O Lord." For our light is not from ourselves; but "You will light my candle, O Lord." "O my God, You will enlighten my darkness." For we through our sins are darkness; but "You, O my God, will enlighten my darkness." (*Exposition on Psalm 18*, no. 29)

Prayers Adoring the
Incarnate Christ

THE INCARNATION HAS been rightly referred to as the linch-pin that holds Christianity together. With the advent of Jesus Christ, light drove away darkness. The birth of our Savior meant that God dwelled in human flesh, the God-man, and an unthinkable event became reality.

St. Augustine focused each of his sermons for the an-nual Feast of the Nativity on a different aspect of the Incarnation, an event riddled with paradoxes. Central among the paradoxes is the mystery of the Christ Himself, fully divine yet fully human, the One who possessed both natures, the One who, though transcendent and eternal, for us subjected Himself to the limitations of time and space. Before we look at prayers devoted to the Incarnate Christ, let's look briefly at an excerpt from one of the saint's Christmas sermons:

And so what praises may we speak, what thanks may we give for the love of God, who so loved us that, for our sake, He through whom time was made became in time; that He who is more ancient in age than the world itself became younger than His many servants in the world; that He became man who made man; that He was created from the Mother whom He created, carried by hands that He formed, and nursed at breasts that He filled; that as a speechless infant, the Word, without whom human eloquence is mute, wailed in a manger: such is His love for us. (*Sermon 188*, no. 2)

In some of his prayers, St. Augustine explores the significant role of the Virgin Birth and of the Blessed Virgin Mary, although St. Augustine never refers to her as *theotokos*, God-bearer. In other prayers, he marvels at the humility of Christ and asks God for that same holy attitude. St. Augustine deals with the origin of faith as a natural response to the Incarnation and the relationship between praying and believing. Along with St. Augustine, we kneel before the manger of the Christ Child: O come, let us adore Him!

1

O manifest infirmity, O miraculous humility, in which the whole divinity lay hidden thus! The Mother to whom His infancy was subject, He was ruling with His power; and she at whose breasts He was nursing, He was feeding with His Truth.

May He, who did not despise to take on even our first beginnings, perfect His gifts in us; and may He, who for our sake wished to be made the Son of Man, make us sons of God. (*Sermon 184*, no. 3)

2

Let us, therefore, celebrate even this day most devotedly, and let us adore the Lord Jesus, who lives now in Heaven yet whom those forebears of our Faith adored lying in the inn. Of course, they venerated His potential, which we venerate in its fulfillment. The first believers of the Gentiles adored Him gaping at His Mother's breasts; the Gentiles now adore Him sitting at the right hand of God the Father. (*Sermon 203*, no. 3)

3

Be exalted: You who were enclosed in the womb of Your Mother; You who were made in her whom You made; You who laid in the manger; You who as a tiny infant nursed at her breasts in the natural order of the flesh; You who, carrying the world, were carried by Your Mother; You whom the old man Simeon acknowledged as an infant and praised as great; You whom the widow Anna saw nursing and recognized as omnipotent; You who hungered for our sake, thirsted for our sake, and were weary on the way for our sake (yet is it possible for Bread to hunger, or the Fountain to thirst, or the Way to be weary?); You who endured all these things for our sake; You who slept and yet who "sleeps not, guarding Israel"; finally, You whom Judas sold, whom the Jews bought and yet did not possess; You, seized, bound, whipped, crowned with thorns, suspended on the Cross, pierced by a lance; You, dead; You, buried: "Be exalted above the heavens, O God." (*Sermon 262*, no. 4)

4

"Be exalted," it says, "be exalted above the heavens," because You are God. Take Your seat in Heaven, You who hung on the Cross. You are awaited as the Judge to come, You who, having been awaited, were judged.

Who would believe these things, unless they were done by Him "who raises the needy from the dust and exalts the poor from the filth"? He Himself raises His own needy flesh and "sets it with the princes of His own people," with whom He will judge the living and the dead. He has settled this needy flesh with those to whom He says: "You will take your seat upon twelve thrones, judging the twelve tribes of Israel." Therefore, "be exalted above the heavens, O God." (*Sermon 262*, nos. 5–6)

5

O Food and Bread of angels! From You the angels are filled, from You they are perfectly nourished and never overindulged; from You they have life, from You they have sense, from You they are blessed. Where are You on account of me? In a lowly inn, in swaddling clothes, in a manger. (*Sermon 196*, no. 3)

6

May Christ, the Son of a virgin and the Spouse of virgins, born after the flesh of a virgin womb and wedded after the Spirit in virgin marriage, help us. (*Of Holy Virginity* 2)

7

Prepare thus, Lord, what You are preparing; for You are preparing us for Yourself, and Yourself for us, inasmuch as You are preparing a place both for Yourself in us, and for us in You. For You have said, "Abide in me, and I in you."

As far as each one has been a partaker of You, some less, some more, such will be the diversity of rewards in proportion to the diversity of merits; such will be the multitude of mansions to suit the inequalities among their inmates; but all of them, none the less, eternally living, and endlessly blessed.

Why is it that You go away? Why is it that You come again? If I understand You aright, You withdraw not Yourself either from the place You go from or from the place You come from: You go away by becoming invisible, You come by again becoming manifest to our eyes. But unless

You remain to direct us, how may we still be advancing in goodness of life, how will the place be prepared where we shall be able to dwell in the fullness of joy?

Let what we have said suffice on the words that have been read from the Gospel as far as "I will come again, and receive you to myself." But the meaning of what follows, "That where I am, there you may be also; and whither I go you know, and the way you know," we shall be in a better condition. (*Tractates on the Gospel of John* 68.3)

8

Let us, therefore, say to the Lord as He rises again: "Because You, Lord, are my Hope"; and to the Lord as He ascends: "You have made the Most High Your refuge." For how will we be proud as we lift up our hearts to Him who became humble for our sake so that we may not remain proud? (*Sermon 261*, no. 1)

9

Come then, O Lord, employ Your keys; open, that we may understand. Oh, You tell all things and yet are not believed. You are thought to be a spirit, are touched, are rudely handled, and yet they who touch You hesitate.

You admonish them out of the Scriptures, and yet they do not understand You. Their hearts are closed; open, and enter in. He did so. "Then opened He their understanding." Open, O Lord, open the heart of him who is in doubt concerning Christ. (*Sermon 66 on the New Testament*, no. 5)

10

O saving teaching! O Teacher and Lord of mortals, unto whom death was pledged and passed on in the cup of pride! He would not teach what Himself was not, He would not bid what Himself did not.

I see You, O good Jesus, with the eyes of faith that You have opened for me, as in an assembly of the human race, crying out and saying, "Come unto Me, and learn of Me."

I beseech You, through whom all things were made, O Son of God, and the Same who was made among all things, O Son of Man: to learn what of You, do we come to You? "For that I am meek," says He, "and lowly of heart." (*Of Holy Virginity* 35)

11

Let them hear You, and let them come to You, and let them learn of You to be meek and lowly, who seek Your Mercy and Truth, by living unto You, unto You, not unto themselves.

Let him hear this, the one laboring and laden, who is weighed down by his burden so as not to dare to lift up his eyes to Heaven, that sinner beating his breast and drawing near from afar.

Let him hear, the centurion, not worthy that You should enter under his roof. Let him hear, Zaccheus, chief of tax collectors, restoring fourfold the gains of damnable sins. Let her hear, the woman in the city a sinner, by so much the more full of tears at Your feet, the more alien she had been from Your steps.

Let them hear, the harlots and tax collectors, who enter into the Kingdom of Heaven before the Scribes and Pharisees. Let them hear, every kind of such ones, feastings with whom were cast in Your teeth as a charge, indeed, as though by whole persons who sought not a physician, whereas You came not to call the righteous but sinners to repentance.

All these, when they are converted unto You, easily grow meek and are humbled before You, mindful of their own most unrighteous life and of Your most indulgent mercy, in that, "where sin has abounded, grace has abounded more." (*Of Holy Virginity* 36)

12

O Lord, our Mediator, God above us, Man for us, I own Your mercy! For because You, who are so great, are troubled through the goodwill of Your love, You preserve, by the richness of Your comfort, the many in Your body who are troubled by the continual experience of their own weakness from perishing utterly in their despair. (*Tractates on the Gospel of John* 52.2)

13

O Lord our God, what is that which You said, "If you believe not that I am?" For what is there that belongs not to the things You have made?

Does not Heaven so belong? Does not the earth? Does not everything in earth and Heaven? Does not man himself to whom You speak? Does not the angel whom You send?

If all these are things made by You, what is that existence You have retained as something exclusively Your own, which You have given to none besides, that You might be such Yourself alone?

For how do I hear "I am who am," as if there were none besides? And how do I hear "If you believe not that I am?" For had they no existence who heard Him? Yes, although they were sinners, they were men. What then can I do?

What that existence is, let Him tell my heart; let Him tell, let Him declare it within; let the inner man hear, the mind apprehend this true existence; for such existence is always unvarying in character. (*Tractates on the Gospel of John* 38.10)

14

Tell me, O my Lord, what to say to Your servants, my fellow servants. The Apostle Thomas had You before him in order to ask You questions, and yet he could not understand You unless he had You within him; I ask You because I know that You are over me; and I ask, seeking, as far as I can, to let my soul diffuse itself in that same region over me where I may listen to You, who use no external sound to convey Your teaching.

Tell me, I pray, how it is that You go to Yourself. Did You formerly leave Yourself to come to us, especially as You came not of Yourself but the Father sent You? I know, indeed, that You emptied Yourself; but in taking the form of a servant, it was neither that You laid down the form of God as something to return to or that You lost it as something to be recovered; and yet You came, and You placed Yourself not only before the carnal eyes but even in the very hands of men. And how otherwise save in Your flesh?

By means of this You came, yet abiding where You were; by this means You returned, without leaving the place to which You had come. If, then, by such means You came and return, by such means doubtless You are not only the way for us to come to You but were the way also for Yourself to come and to return. For when You returned to the life that You are Yourself, then of a truth, that same flesh of Yours You brought from death unto life. (*Tractates on the Gospel of John* 69.3)

15

Let the words of God seize upon your hearts, and let Him whose you are claim His own possession, that is, your minds, that they not be turned aside to anything else.

Let each one of you so be entirely here that he be not here; that is, let him give himself wholly to the Word of God, which sounds on earth, that by it he may be lifted up and not be on earth.

For therefore was He "God with us," that we might be with Him. For He who came down from Heaven to be with us makes us ascend to Him, so that we may be with Him. Meanwhile, He scorned not our estrangement; for nowhere is He a stranger, who made all things. (*Exposition on Psalm 146*, no.1)

16

Glory to our Lord, and to the Mercy of the Same, and to the Truth of the Same, because neither has He forsaken by mercy to make us blessed through His Grace nor defrauded us of truth: because first Truth veiled in flesh came to us and healed through His flesh the interior eye of our heart, in order that hereafter face to face we may be able to see it.

Giving thanks, therefore, to Him, let us say with the same psalm the last verses, which sometime since, too, I have said: "Be exalted above the Heavens, O God, and above all the earth Your glory." (*Exposition on Psalm 57*, no. 17)

17

"Be exalted, O Lord, in Your strength." Lord, whom in humiliation they did not discern, be exalted in Your strength, which they thought weakness. "We will sing and praise Your power." In heart and in deed we will celebrate and make known Your marvels. (*Exposition on Psalm 21*, no. 14)

Prayers for Forgiveness
and Salvation

"His Cross hath brought us mercy" (*Exposition on Psalm 63*, no. 13) — these words of St. Augustine could easily serve as the refrain for all the prayers in this section, which focuses on prayers that emphasize divine forgiveness and salvation.

Characterized by humility and contrition, St. Augustine's prayers convey a profound understanding of our total dependence on God. Recurrent themes include the restorative, redemptive acts of God, the cleansing nature of divine grace, the incomprehensible goodness of God, and the sufficiency of Christ's sacrifice for the salvation of the world.

Powerfully written, every prayer resounds with hope, for "by hope we are saved" (*Confessions* 11.9.11). Grounded in Scripture, the prayers call to our attention the words of the psalmist, "Hide not Thy face from us" (see Ps. 27:9 (26:9 Douay-Rheims)) — words that St. Augustine recalls in perhaps his most memorable phrase in this section: "Let me die, lest I die, if only I may see Your face" (*Confessions* 1.5.5).

St. Augustine does not presume that God owes him anything. His prayers in this section display that deep humility. May these prayers inspire us all to long for a contrite heart.

1

May He cleanse us with His grace. May He cleanse us with His help and with His comfort. (*Sermon 261*, no. 9)

2

Christ, wash us. "Forgive us our debts," because our love is not altogether extinguished: for "we also forgive our debtors." When we listen to You, the bones that have been humbled rejoice with You in the heavenly places.

But when we preach You, we have to tread the ground in order to open to You: and then, if we are blameworthy, we are troubled; if we are commended, we become inflated.

Wash our feet that were formerly cleansed but have again been defiled in our walking through the earth to open unto You. Let this be enough today, beloved.

But in whatever we have happened to offend, by saying otherwise than we ought, or have been unduly elated by your commendations, entreat that our feet may be washed, and may your prayers find acceptance with God. (*Tractates on the Gospel of John* 57.6)

3

O Medicine, looking after all: compressing all that was swollen, restoring all that had wasted away, trimming all that was excess, keeping all that is necessary, renewing all that was destroyed, correcting all that was deformed!

Who now can raise himself against the Son of God?

Who can give up hope of his salvation, when the Son of God wished to be so humbled for his sake?

Who can think that a happy life is found in those things that the Son of God taught must be despised?

Who can fall to adversities, when he believes that in the Son of God the nature of man has been preserved against such persecutions?

Who can think that the Kingdom of Heaven is closed to him, when he knows that tax collectors and prostitutes have imitated the Son of God?

What wickedness can there possibly be in he who contemplates, cherishes, and closely follows the deeds and words of that Man, in whom the Son of God has revealed Himself to us as an example of life? (*The Christian Combat* 11)

4

To these cry out, let these hear You, in that You are "meek and lowly of heart." Let these, by how much they are great, by so much humble themselves in all things, that they may find grace before You.

They are just: but they are not, are they, such as You, justifying the ungodly? They are chaste: but their mothers nurtured them in sin in their wombs. They are holy, but You are also the Holy of Holies. They are virgins, but they are not also born of virgins. They are wholly chaste both in spirit and in flesh, but they are not the Word made flesh.

And yet let them learn not from those unto whom You forgive sins but from You Yourself, the Lamb of God who takes away the sins of the world, in that You are "meek and lowly of heart." (*Of Holy Virginity 37*)

5

Let us give thanks to our Lord and Savior, who has healed us of our wounds without any previous merits of ours, has reconciled us who were His enemies, has redeemed us from captivity, led us back to light from darkness, and called us back to life from death. And humbly confessing our sins, let us beg His mercy, so that, because, as the psalmist said, "His mercy precedes us," He may choose not only to preserve His gifts or graces in us but also to increase them, which He Himself has deemed worthy to give; who with the Father and the Holy Spirit lives and reigns forever and ever. Amen. (*Sermon 333*, no. 7)

6

Lord, you know that I have not sinned against my brother but rather he has sinned against me. And You know that he has harmed himself because he sinned against me, and because if I should come to him, he would not seek forgiveness from me. With good intention, I ask that you forgive him. (*Sermon 211*, no. 5)

7

Oh! How shall I find rest in You? Who will send You into my heart to inebriate it, so that I may forget my woes and embrace You, my only good?

What are You to me? Have compassion on me, that I may speak. What am I to You that You demand my love, and unless I give it You are angry and threaten me with great sorrows?

Is it, then, a light sorrow not to love You? Alas! Alas! Tell me of Your compassion, O Lord my God, what You are to me. "Say unto my soul, I am your salvation." So speak that I may hear. Behold, Lord, the ears of my heart are before You; open them, and "say unto my soul, I am your salvation." When I hear, may I run and lay hold on You. Hide not Your face from me. Let me die, lest I die, if only I may see Your face.

Cramped is the dwelling of my soul; expand it, that You may enter in. It is in ruins; restore it. There is that about it that must offend Your eyes; I confess and know it, but who will cleanse it? Or to whom shall I cry but to

You? Cleanse me from my secret sins, O Lord, and keep Your servant from those of other men.

I believe, and therefore do I speak: Lord, You know. Have I not confessed my transgressions to You, O my God; and You have put away the iniquity of my heart?

I do not contend in judgment with You, who are the Truth; and I would not deceive myself, lest my iniquity lie against itself. I do not, therefore, contend in judgment with You, for "if You, Lord, should mark iniquities, O Lord, who shall stand?" (*Confessions* 1.5.5–6)

8

Hearken, O God! Alas for the sins of men! Man says this, and You have compassion on him; for You created him, but You did not create the sin that is in him.

Who brings to my remembrance the sin of my infancy? For before You none is free from sin, not even the infant who has lived but a day upon the earth. Who brings this to my remembrance? Does not each little one, in whom I behold that which I do not remember of myself?

In what, then, did I sin? Is it that I cried for the breast? If I should now so cry — not indeed for the breast but for the food suitable to my years — I should be most justly laughed at and rebuked. What I then did deserved rebuke; but as I could not understand those who rebuked me, neither custom nor reason suffered me to be rebuked. For as we grow, we root out and cast from us such habits.

I have not seen anyone who is wise, when "purging" anything, cast away the good. Or was it good, even for a time, to strive to get by crying that which, if given, would be hurtful—for the infant to be bitterly indignant that those who were free, and his elders, and those to whom he owed his being, besides many others wiser than he who would not give way to the nod of his good pleasure, were not subject to him—to endeavor to harm, by struggling as much as he could, because those commands were not obeyed that only could have been obeyed to his hurt?

Then, in the weakness of the infant's limbs, and not in his will, lies his innocence. I myself have seen and known an infant to be jealous although he could not speak. He became pale and cast bitter looks on his foster-brother.

Who is ignorant of this? Mothers and nurses tell us that they appease these things by I know not what remedies; and may this be taken for innocence, that when the fountain of milk is flowing fresh and abundant, one who has need should not be allowed to share it, though he needs that nourishment to sustain life? Yet we look leniently on these things, not because they are not faults, nor because the faults are small, but because they will vanish as age increases. For although You may allow these things now, You could not bear them with equanimity if found in an older person.

You, therefore, O Lord my God, who gave life to the infant, and a frame that, as we see, You have endowed with senses, compacted with limbs, beautified with form, and, for its general good and safety, has introduced all vital energies—You command me to praise You for these things, "to give thanks unto the Lord, and to sing praise unto Your name, O Most High"; for You are a God omnipotent and good, though You had done nought but these things that none other can do but You, who alone made all things, O You most fair, who made all things fair and orders all according to Your law.

This period, then, of my life, O Lord, of which I have no remembrance, which I believe on the word of others, and which I guess from other infants, it chagrins me—true though the guess be—to reckon in this life of mine that I lead in this world; inasmuch as, in the darkness of my forgetfulness, it is like to that which I passed in my mother's womb. But if "I was shapen in iniquity, and in sin did my mother conceive me," where, I pray you, O my God, where, Lord, or when was I, Your servant, innocent? But behold, I pass by that time, for what have I to do with that, the memories of which I cannot recall? (*Confessions* 1.7.11–12)

9

I will love You, O Lord, and thank You, and confess unto Your name, because You have put away from me these so wicked and nefarious acts of mine.

To Your grace I attribute it, and to Your mercy, that You have melted away my sin as it were ice. To Your grace also I attribute whatsoever of evil I have not committed; for what might I not have committed, loving as I did the sin for the sin's sake?

Yes, all I confess to have been pardoned me, both those which I committed by my own perverseness and those which, by Your guidance, I committed not. (*Confessions* 2.7.15)

10

For Your hands, O my God, in the hidden design of Your Providence, did not desert my soul; and out of the blood of my mother's heart, through the tears that she poured out by day and by night, was a sacrifice offered to You for me; and by marvellous ways did You deal with me.

It was You, O my God, who did it, for the steps of a man are ordered by the Lord, and He shall dispose his way. Or how can we procure salvation but from Your hand, remaking what it has made? (*Confessions* 5.7.13)

11

In this Beginning, O God, have You made Heaven and earth — in Your Word, in Your Son, in Your Power, in Your Wisdom, in Your Truth, wondrously speaking and wondrously making.

Who shall comprehend? Who shall relate it? What is that which shines through me and strikes my heart without injury, and I both shudder and burn? I shudder inasmuch as I am unlike it; and I burn inasmuch as I am like it.

It is Wisdom itself that shines through me, clearing my cloudiness, which again overwhelms me, fainting from it, in the darkness and amount of my punishment.

For my strength is brought down in need, so that I cannot endure my blessings, until You, O Lord, who have been gracious to all my iniquities, heal also all my infirmities; because You shall also redeem my life from corruption, crown me with Your loving kindness and mercy, and satisfy my desire with good things, because my youth shall be renewed like the eagle's.

For by hope we are saved; and through patience we await Your promises. Let him that is able hear You discoursing within. I will with confidence cry out from Your oracle, "How wonderful are Your works, O Lord! In Wisdom have You made them all." And this Wisdom is the Beginning, and in that Beginning, You have made Heaven and earth. (*Confessions* 11.9.11)

12

I call upon You, my God, my mercy, who made me and who did not forget me, though I am forgetful of You. I call You into my soul, which by the desire that You inspire in it, You prepare for Your reception.

Do not forsake me calling upon You, who anticipated me before I called and importunately urged with manifold calls that I should hear You from afar, and be converted, and call upon You who called me. For You, O Lord, have blotted out all my evil deserts so that You might not repay into my hands wherewith I have fallen from You, and You have anticipated all my good deserts so that You might repay into Your hands wherewith You made me; because before I was, You were, nor was I anything to which You might grant being. And yet behold, I am, out of Your goodness, anticipating all this that You have made me and of which You have made me.

For neither had You stood in need of me, nor am I such a good as to be helpful to You, my Lord and God; not that I may so serve You as though You were fatigued in working, or lest Your power may be less if lacking my assistance, nor that, like the land, I may so cultivate You that You would be uncultivated did I cultivate You not, but that I may serve and worship You to the end that I may have wellbeing from You; from whom it is that I am one susceptible of wellbeing. (*Confessions* 13.1.1)

13

And yet I erred, O Lord God, the Creator and Disposer of all things in Nature—but of sin the Disposer only—I erred, O Lord my God, in doing contrary to the wishes of my parents and of those masters; for this learning that they (no matter for what motive) wished me to acquire, I might have put to good account afterward. For I disobeyed them not because I had chosen a better way but from a fondness for play, loving the honor of victory in the matches, and to have my ears tickled with lying fables, in order that they might itch the more furiously—the same curiosity beaming more and more in my eyes for the shows and sports of my elders.

Yet those who give these entertainments are held in such high repute that almost all desire the same for their children, whom they are still willing should be beaten if these same games keep them from the studies by which they desire them to arrive at, being the givers of them.

Look down upon these things, O Lord, with compassion, and deliver us who now call upon You; deliver those also who do not call upon You, that they may call upon You, and that You may deliver them. (*Confessions* 1.10.16)

14

"And in Your name I will lift up my hands." Lift up, therefore, your hands in prayer. Our Lord has lifted up for us His hands on the Cross, and His hands were stretched out for us, and therefore His hands were stretched out on the Cross in order that our hands might be stretched out unto good works, because His Cross has brought us mercy.

Behold, He has lifted up His hands and has offered Himself for us as a Sacrifice to God, and through that Sacrifice, all our sins have been effaced.

Let us also lift up our hands to God in prayer: and our hands, being lifted up to God, shall not be confounded if they are exercised in good works. (*Exposition on Psalm 63*, no. 13)

Prayers of Petition

THIS IS THE longest section of all, as all of St. Augustine's prayers naturally include petitions. While there is some overlap with other themes in this collection, I chose to group these prayers together because their pervasive theme is petitionary prayer.

These prayers are eloquent, profound, and deeply stirring. The saint unselfishly asks for an increase in faith, wisdom, and love. He asks for protection from evil and temptation and, ever conscious of his role as bishop and shepherd, prays not only for himself but for others: "Let Your favor be ever present with Your Holy Catholic Church" (*Meditations* 1.39).

Some prayers include beautiful metaphors, such as "Draw this thirsty soul to the rivers of eternal pleasure, to the fountain of living water, that I may drink my fill, and live forever, O God of my life" (*Meditations* 1.36). Ultimately, of course, St. Augustine longs for nothing less than Christ Himself, as the saint explains: "The object of our desires is He Himself" (*Exposition on Psalm 43*, no. 2).

These prayers are moving and memorable even today, as we are reminded of the liturgy as we read prayers such as "O Lord God, grant Your peace unto us" (*Confessions* 13.35.50) and "Heal me, Blessed Physician of souls, and so shall I be healed" (*Meditations* 1.35).

This section also contains one of the saint's briefest prayers of all, yet it is one that contains a request characteristic of the wisdom of Solomon and Plato: "God, always the same, let me know myself, let me know You! The prayer is made" (*Soliloquies* 2.1).

May the wisdom of these petitionary prayers enlighten our minds and inflame our hearts with St. Augustine's desire for the Living God.

1

Behold, my Lord God, I have given; behold in the sight of You and Your angels, and in the sight of all Your people, I have paid out Your money; for I fear Your judgment.

I have given; exact payment, O God!

Even if I should not speak, You will exact payment. Therefore, I say this instead: I have given.

Convert and spare me, O God! Make pure those who were impure, so that at the same time in your sight, when the judgment comes, we may rejoice, both the one who has paid and the one to whom it has been paid. (*Sermon 132*, no. 4)

2

O Lord Jesus, the anointed of God, the Word of the Father, who came into the world on purpose to save sinners!... Let "me cease to do evil, learn to do well," and reduce all my actions to rule and due order; take away from me "whatsoever is offensive" to You and hurtful to myself, and implant in me all those virtues and graces that may conduce to my soul's advantage and Your good liking and acceptance of me. "Who can bring a clean thing out of an unclean" but You alone? You are a God infinite in goodness and power, "justifying the ungodly, quickening them that lay dead in trespasses and sins," changing the hearts of men and forming them into new and different creatures. Your eyes behold my many and great imperfections; look down upon them with an eye of pity, send down Your hand of compassion from above, and remove far from me whatever is displeasing in Your sight. My spiritual health and diseases are both in Your sight. O strengthen, I beseech You, and preserve the former, and in much mercy, heal the latter.

"Heal me, Blessed Physician of souls, and so I shall be healed"; hold me up, almighty Preserver of men, and so shall I be safe. You who "give medicines for the cure of our sickness" and sustain that health that is Your own; You who repair our breaches and build up our decayed ruins with a word of Your mouth. If You think fit (as I hope You will) to sow the good seed in Your field my heart, the first part of that blessed work must be to prepare and correct the soil by rooting out the weeds and thorns of vicious habits and dispositions that will choke the work and make it unfruitful. (*Meditations* 1.35)

3

O sweetest, kindest, dearest Jesus! Pour into me, I beg You, the abundance of Your love so that there may be no remains of earthly or sensual desires or thoughts in my breast, but You and Your love may reign unrivalled there and possess my heart entirely. Write Your name in my mind so that You and Your commands may be ever before my eyes. Kindle in my soul that holy fire that You have

sent into the world so that it may melt away my dross
and qualify me for offering to You the daily sacrifice of a
broken and contrite spirit.

Sweetest Redeemer, as You have given me the sincere
desire, so give me the attainment of Your chaste and holy
love, fervent as my desire and entire as the sincerity with
which I ask it. "Let my head be waters, and my eyes a
fountain of tears," that these may speak for me and testify
the greatness of my love and the inward delights I feel,
too big to be contained within my heart and perpetually
running over in tears of joy. (*Meditations* 1.35)

4

I frequently call to mind the devout addresses of Your
servant Hannah, who came to Your tabernacle to beg
a son from You: and, upon each remembrance of her
remarkable piety and perseverance in prayers, I find myself tormented with grief and confounded with shame
for my own coldness and deadness in devotion. For if
she did not only weep but continued weeping in hopes
of obtaining a son, what affectionate complaints, what
measure of tears become my soul, which comes to You
in prayer, which seeks and loves my God and Savior,

desiring to receive Him and to be received by Him? What sighs and groanings, what earnest gaspings, what impatient thirstings ought I to bring who am in pursuit of my God day and night and desire to love and to enjoy nothing but Him only?

O look, then, upon me and extend Your mercy to me, for the "sorrows of my heart are enlarged." Permit me to taste of Your heavenly comforts, and do not disdain that sinful soul for which You did not grudge to die. Give me plenteousness of tears flowing from an affectionate heart, such as, by lamenting, may prevail for forgiveness of my sins, a release from the bands with which I have so long been tired, and a godly sorrow that may produce spiritual and heavenly joy, so that, if I cannot rise to that exalted pitch of zeal with some illustrious martyrs and confessors and eminently devout men whose bright examples I despair of coming up with, I may however ... be admitted to a share in Your Kingdom with devout women. (*Meditations* 1.35)

5

I entreat You, for Your own sake, and for the glory of Your holy Name, to grant me such a tender and affectionate sense of Your goodness, and my own unworthiness, that every time I think, or speak, or read, or write of, upon every remembrance of, every approach to my God and Savior, in the sacrifices of prayer and praise, my eyes may overflow with tears of remorse and love. You, the King of glory, the teacher and pattern of all virtues, have instructed us to weep, both by Your Word and by Your own example. You have said, "Blessed are they that mourn, for they shall be comforted," and You Yourself shed tears of compassion for Your deceased friend, and yet more abundantly for the ungracious city of Your people, and its approaching destruction.

By Your most precious tears, and by all the wonderful instances of Your mercy for the relief of lost mankind, I beg the grace of tears and godly sorrow, which my soul vehemently thirsts after. I cannot attain to this unless You vouchsafe to give it me; for it is Your Holy Spirit alone that can bring water out of this rock and soften the hearts of hardened sinners. This You have been pleased to communicate freely to many primitive and eminent saints, whose pious footsteps I dare to tread in. Send down Your former and Your latter rain, and water this dry soil with the dew of Heaven so that I may with true compunction bewail my sin and misery; and kindle in my heart a fervent zeal so that I may be a burnt offering to You, a sacrifice of sweet savor in Your presence. And let my tears wash that polluted offering so that it may be presented clean and pure. For of these I shall still have daily need; because, though by the assistance of Your grace I consecrate myself never so devoutly and entirely to Your service, yet such is my frailty, that still in "many things" I shall "offend." Grant me, therefore, this necessary grace so that I may taste of Your cup, and quench my thirst so that my soul may ever pant after You and burn with the love of You alone, regardless of any other object and getting above the vanities of sense and miseries of the world.

Hear me, my God; hearken, Light of my eyes, grant me my request; and grant me to ask such things as You delight to give. Let not my manifold offenses stop the current of Your grace, whose property it is to be a "God hearing prayer," and always to have mercy. But "according to the multitude of Your mercies do away my offenses, and think upon me, O Lord, for Your goodness." (*Meditations* 1.35)

6

O Lord, hear us. Make us for that You have made us. Make us good, for that You have made us enlightened men. These white-robed, enlightened ones hear Your word by me. For enlightened by Your grace they stand before You. "This is the day that the Lord has made."

Only let them labor, let them pray for this, that when these days shall have gone by, they may not become darkness, who have been made the light of the wonders and the blessings of God. (*Sermon 70 on the New Testament*, no. 3)

8

Turning, then, to the Lord our God, the Father Almighty, in purity of heart, let us render unto Him, as our frailty best can, our highest and abundant thanks, with our whole mind praying His singular goodness, that in His good pleasure He would vouchsafe to hear our prayers, that by His Power He would drive out the enemy from our deeds and thoughts, would enlarge our faith, direct our minds, grant us spiritual thoughts, and bring us safe to His endless blessedness, through His Son Jesus Christ. Amen. (*Sermon 17 on the New Testament*, no. 10)

9

"Because with You, O God, is the fountain of life, and You will let them drink from the rushing streams of Your delight." From where? "Because with You, O Lord, is the fountain of life, and in Your Light we will see light."

The Spirit of God is both drink and light. If you were to come upon a fountain in the dark, you would light a lamp to reach it. But you do not need to light a lamp at the Fountain of Light: it shines for you itself, and it leads you to itself. When you come to drink, approach and be illuminated. "Approach Him, and be illuminated." Do not withdraw, or else you will be swallowed in darkness.

Lord God, call them, and let them approach you: strengthen them so that they do not withdraw. Make Your new sons into old men from their infancy, but not from old men into dead men. For one may grow old in this wisdom, but one may not die in it. *(Sermon 225, no. 4, given on Easter Sunday to the newly baptized)*

10

Inspire my soul, O Lord my God, with a holy desire of You, my chief, my only good, that I may so earnestly desire as diligently to seek You, so successfully seek as to be happy in finding You; make me so sensible of that happiness in finding as most passionately to love You; so effectually to express that love as to make some amends for my past wickedness, by hating and forsaking my former evil courses and entering upon a conversation exemplarily pious for the time to come.

Give me, dear God, hearty repentance, a humble and contrite spirit; make my eyes a fountain of tears and my hands liberal dispensers of alms, and unwearied instruments of good works. You are my King; reign absolute in my heart, subdue and expel thence all rebellious passions; quench all the impure burnings of fleshly lusts, and kindle in it the bright fire of Your love.

You are my Redeemer: beat down and drive out the spirit of pride and impart to me, in much mercy, the treasure of Your own unexampled humility and wonderful condescension.

You are my Savior, take from me the rage of anger; and arm me, I beseech You, with the shield of patience.

You are my Creator, root out from me all that rancor and malice by which my nature is corrupted; and implant in me all that sweetness and gentleness of temper that may render me a man made in Your own image and after the likeness of Your own divine goodness.

You are my most merciful and indulgent Father. O grant Your own child those best of gifts: a firm and right faith, a steadfast and well-grounded hope, and a never failing charity. (*Meditations* 1.1)

11

"O Father of lights, from whom every good thing comes," enrich me, I beseech You, with this, I ask no other treasure: let this be my introduction into Your presence; this my defense against the assaults of spiritual enemies; this my fountain of tears to quench the flames of sin; this my sure retreat from the fury of inordinate passions and desires.

Suffer me not, O strength of my soul's health, suffer me not, I beg, to be one of those weak Christians who for "a time believe, and in time of temptation fall away." But cover my head in the day of battle; for You, You only are my hope in the day of trouble, and my safety in the time of danger. (*Meditations* 1.2)

12

And now, O Holy Spirit, love of God, who proceeds from the Almighty Father and His most Blessed Son, powerful advocate, and sweetest comforter, infuse Your grace, and descend plentifully into my heart; enlighten the dark corners of this neglected dwelling, and scatter there Your cheerful beams! Dwell in that soul that longs to be Your temple; water that barren soil, overrun with weeds and briars, and lost for want of cultivating, and make it fruitful with Your dew from Heaven.

Come, glory and crown of the living and only safeguard of the dying. Come, Holy Spirit, in much mercy, come, make me fit to receive You, and condescend to my infirmities, that my meanness may not be disdained by Your greatness nor my weakness by Your strength: all that I beg for the sake of Jesus Christ, my only Savior, who in the unity of You, O Holy Spirit, lives and reigns with the Father, one God, world without end. Amen. (*Meditations* 1.9)

13

My hope, my Christ, my God, Savior and lover of men, Light and Way, Life and Health, Glory and Grace of all that love and serve You! Look down from the throne of Your majesty, and in the midst of bliss, remember the injuries and sufferings, the scourges, and the Cross, the wounds and death that You endured—and think with favor on Your suppliant, for whose sake You were pleased to endure and do so much. (*Meditations* 1.18)

14

Turning to the Lord God, the Father Almighty, let us pour out to Him fullest and abundant thanks from a pure heart, as much as our littleness can, begging His singular clemency with all our soul, that He will think it worthy to hear our prayers in His good will, drive out the enemy from our actions and thoughts by means of His virtue, increase our faith, govern our minds, grant us spiritual thoughts, and lead us to His own blessedness, through Jesus Christ His Son, Amen. (*Sermon 67*, no. 10)

15

O God, our Father, who exhorts us to pray and grants what we ask, if we are better and live better when we pray to You, listen to me, groping amid these shadows, and stretch out to me Your right hand! Hold Your Light before me! Call me back from wandering! Under Your guidance, let me return to myself, let me return to You! Amen. (*Soliloquies* 2.6)

16

God, always the same, let me know myself, let me know You! The prayer is made. (*Soliloquies* 2.1)

17

Thanks be to You, my joy, my pride, my confidence, my God—thanks be to You for Your gifts; but preserve them to me. For thus will You preserve me; and those things that You have given me shall be developed and perfected, and I myself shall be with You, for from You is my being. (*Confessions* 1.20.31)

18

You have taught me, good Father, that "unto the pure all things are pure"; but "it is evil for that man who eats with offense"; and that "every creature of Yours is good, and nothing to be refused, if it be received with, thanksgiving"; and that "meat commends us not to God"; and that no man should "judge us in meat or in drink"; and that he who eats, let him not despise him who eats not; and let not him who eats not judge him who eats.

These things have I learned, thanks and praise be unto You, O my God and Master, who knocks at my ears and enlightens my heart; deliver me out of all temptation. (*Confessions* 10.31.46)

19

O Lord, since eternity is Yours, are You ignorant of the things that I say unto You? Or do You see at the time that which comes to pass in time? Why, therefore, do I place before You so many relations of things? Not surely so that You might know them through me, but so that I may awaken my own love and that of my readers toward

You, that we may all say, "Great is the Lord, and greatly to be praised."

I have already said, and shall say, for the love of Your love I do this. For we also pray, and yet Truth says, "Your Father knows what things you have need of before you ask Him."

Therefore, we make our love for You known in confessing to You our own miseries and Your mercies upon us, so that You may free us altogether, since You have begun, so that we may cease to be wretched in ourselves, and so that we may be blessed in You; since You have called us, so that we may be poor in spirit, and meek, and mourners, and hungering and thirsty after righteousness, and merciful, and pure in heart, and peacemakers.

Behold, I have told You many things, which I could and which I would, for You first would have me confess unto You, the Lord my God, for You are good, since Your "mercy endures forever." (*Confessions* 11.1.1)

20

O Lord my God, "hear my prayer," and let Your mercy regard my longing, since it burns not for myself alone but because it desires to benefit brotherly charity; and You see into my heart, that it is so.

I would sacrifice to You the service of my thought and tongue; and You give what I may offer unto You. For "I am poor and needy," but "You are rich unto all that call upon You," and You who are free from care, care for us.

Circumcise from all rashness and from all lying my inward and outward lips. Let Your Scriptures be my chaste delights. Neither let me be deceived in them nor deceive out of them.

O Lord, hear and pity; O Lord my God, light of the blind and strength of the weak; even also light of those that see and strength of the strong, hearken unto my soul, and hear it crying "out of the depths."

For unless Your ears are present in the depths also, where shall we go? Where shall we cry? "The day is Yours, and the night also is Yours." At Your nod the moments flee by.

Grant space for our meditations among the hidden things of Your law, and do not close it against us who knock. For not in vain have You willed that the obscure secret of so many pages should be written. Nor is it that those forests have not their harts, betaking themselves therein, and ranging, and walking, and feeding, lying down, and ruminating.

Perfect me, O Lord, and reveal them unto me. Behold, Your voice is my joy, Your voice surpasses the abundance of pleasures. Give that which I love, for I do love; and this have You given. Abandon not Your own gifts, nor despise Your grass that thirsts.

Let me confess unto You whatsoever I shall have found in Your books, and let me hear the voice of praise, and let me imbibe You and reflect on the wonderful things of Your law; even from the beginning, wherein You made the Heaven and the earth, unto the everlasting Kingdom of Your holy city that is with You.

Lord, have mercy on me and hear my desire. For I think that it is not of the earth, nor of gold and silver and precious stones, nor gorgeous apparel, nor honors and powers, nor the pleasures of the flesh, nor necessaries for the body, and this life of our pilgrimage; all which are added to those that seek Your Kingdom and Your righteousness.

Behold, O Lord my God, where my desire is from. The unrighteous have told me of delights, but not such as Your law, O Lord. Behold where my desire is from. Behold, Father, look and see, and approve; and let it be pleasing in the sight of Your mercy, that I may find grace before You, that the secret things of Your Word may be opened unto me when I knock.

I beseech, by our Lord Jesus Christ, Your Son, "the Man of Your right hand, the Son of Man, whom You made strong for Yourself," as Your Mediator and ours, through whom You have sought us, although not seeking You, but sought us that we might seek You — Your Word through whom You have made all things, and among them me also, Your Only-begotten, through whom You have called to adoption the believing people, and therein me also. I beseech You through Him, who sits at Your right hand, and "makes intercession for us," "in whom are hid all treasures of wisdom and knowledge." Him do I seek in Your books. Of Him did Moses write; this says Himself; this says the Truth. (*Confessions* 11.2.3–4)

21

My heart, O Lord, affected by the words of Your Holy Scripture, is much busied in this poverty of my life; and therefore, for the most part, is the want of human intelligence copious in language, because inquiry speaks more than discovery, and because demanding is longer than obtaining, and the hand that knocks is more active than the hand that receives.

We hold the promise; who shall break it? "If God is for us, who can be against us?" "Ask, and you shall have; seek, and you shall find; knock, and it shall be opened unto you: for every one that asks receives; and he that seeks finds; and to him that knocks, it shall be opened."

These are Your own promises; and who need fear to be deceived where the Truth promises? (*Confessions* 12.1.1)

22

Oh, let Truth, the light of my heart, not my own darkness, speak unto me! I have descended to that and am darkened. But there, even there, did I love You. I went astray and remembered You. I heard Your voice behind me bidding me return, and scarcely did I hear it for the tumults of the unquiet ones.

And now, behold, I return burning and panting after Your fountain. Let no one prohibit me; of this will I drink, and so have life. Let me not be my own life; from myself have I badly lived — death was I unto myself; in You do I revive. Speak unto me; discourse unto me. In Your books have I believed, and their words are very deep. (*Confessions* 12.10.10)

23

Already have You told me, O Lord, with a strong voice, in my inner ear, that You are eternal, having alone immortality, since You are not changed by any shape or motion, nor is Your will altered by times, because no will that changes is immortal.

This in Your sight is clear to me, and let it become more and more clear, I beseech You; and in that manifestation, let me abide more soberly under Your wings. Likewise have You said to me, O Lord, with a strong voice, in my inner ear, that You have made all natures and substances, which are not what You are Yourself, and yet they are; and that only is not from You that is not, and the motion of the will from You who are, to that which in a less degree is, because such motion is guilt and sin; and that no one's sin does either hurt You or disturb the order of Your rule, either first or last. This, in Your sight, is clear to me, and let it become more and more clear, I beseech You; and in that manifestation, let me abide more soberly under Your wings.

Likewise have You said to me, with a strong voice, in my inner ear, that that creature, whose will You alone are, is not coeternal unto You, and that, with a most persevering purity drawing its support from You, does, in place and at no time, put forth its own mutability; and Yourself being ever present with it, unto whom with its entire affection it holds itself, having no future to expect nor conveying into the past what it remembers, is varied by no change, nor extended into any times.

O blessed one — if any such there be — in clinging unto Your Blessedness; blessed in You, its everlasting Inhabitant and its Enlightener! Nor do I find what the Heaven of heavens, which is the Lord's, can be better called than Your house, which contemplates Your delight without any defection of going forth to another; a pure mind, most peacefully one, by that stability of peace of holy spirits, the citizens of Your city "in the heavenly places," above these heavenly places that are seen.

Whence the soul, whose wandering has been made far away, may understand, if now she thirsts for You, if now her tears have become bread to her, while it is daily said to her "Where is your God?" if she now seeks of You one thing, and desires that she may dwell in Your house all the days of her life.

And what is her life but You? And what are Your days but Your eternity, as Your years that fail not, because You are the same?

Hence, therefore, can the soul, which is able, understand how far beyond all times You are eternal; when Your house, which has not wandered from You, although it be not coeternal with You, yet by continually and unfailingly clinging unto You, suffers no vicissitude of times. This in Your sight is clear to me, and may it become more and more clear to me, I beseech You; and in this manifestation may I abide more soberly under Your wings. (*Confessions* 12.11.11–13)

24

O Lord, who are God, and not flesh and blood, if man does see anything less, can anything lie hidden from "Your good Spirit," who shall "lead me into the land of upright-ness," which You Yourself, by those words, were about to reveal to future readers, although he through whom they were spoken, amid the many interpretations that might have been found, fixed on but one?

Which, if it be so, let that which he thought on be more exalted than the rest. But to us, O Lord, either point out the same or any other true one that may be pleasing to You; so that whether You make known to us that which You did to that man of Yours or some other by occasion of the same words, yet You may feed us, not error deceive us.

Behold, O Lord my God, how many things we have written concerning a few words—how many, I beseech You! What strength of ours, what ages would suffice for all Your books after this manner?

Permit me, therefore, in these more briefly to confess unto You, and to select some one true, certain, and good sense, that You shall inspire, although many senses offer themselves, where many, indeed, I may; this being the faith of my confession, that if I should say that which Your minister felt, rightly and profitably, this I should strive for; the which if I shall not attain, yet I may say that which Your Truth willed through Its words to say unto me, which said also unto him what It willed. (*Confessions* 12.32.43)

25

Who but You, our God, made for us that firmament of authority over us in Your divine Scripture? As it is said, For Heaven shall be folded up like a scroll; and now it is extended over us like a skin.

For Your divine Scripture is of more sublime authority, since those mortals through whom You dispensed it unto us underwent mortality. And You know, O Lord,

You know, how You with skins clothed men when by sin they became mortal.

Whence as a skin have You stretched out the firmament of Your Book; that is to say, Your harmonious words, which by the ministry of mortals You have spread over us. For by their very death is that solid firmament of authority in Your discourses set forth by them more sublimely extended above all things that are under it, the which, while they were living here, was not so eminently extended. You had not as yet spread abroad the Heaven like a skin; You had not as yet announced everywhere the report of their deaths.

Let us look, O Lord, "upon the heavens, the work of Your fingers"; clear from our eyes that mist with which You have covered them. There is that testimony of Yours that gives wisdom unto the little ones. Perfect, O my God, Your praise out of the mouth of babes and sucklings. Nor have we known any other books so destructive to pride, so destructive to the enemy and the defender, who resists Your reconciliation in defense of his own sins.

I know not, O Lord, I know not other such "pure" words that so persuade me to confession and make my neck submissive to Your yoke, and invite me to serve You for nought. Let me understand these things, good Father.

Grant this to me, placed under them; because You have established these things for those placed under them.

Other "waters" there be "above" this "firmament," I believe immortal, and removed from earthly corruption. Let them praise Your Name—those supercelestial people, Your angels, who have no need to look up at this firmament or to attain the knowledge of Your Word by reading—let them praise You. For they always behold Your face, and therein read without any syllables in time what Your eternal will wills.

They read, they choose, they love. They are always reading; and that which they read never passes away. For, by choosing and by loving, they read the very unchangeableness of Your counsel. Their book is not closed, nor is the scroll folded up, because You Yourself are this to them, yes, and are so eternally; because You have appointed them above this firmament, which You have made firm over the weakness of the lower people, where they might look up and learn Your mercy, announcing in time You who have made times.

"For Your mercy, O Lord, is in the heavens, and Your faithfulness reaches unto the clouds." The clouds pass away, but the Heaven remains. The preachers of Your Word pass away from this life into another; but Your Scripture is spread abroad over the people, even to the end of the world. Yes, both "Heaven and earth shall pass away, but Your Words shall not pass away." Because the scroll shall be rolled together, and the grass over which it was spread shall with its goodliness pass away; but "Your Word remains forever," which now appears unto us in the dark image of the clouds, and through the glass of the heavens, not as it is; and we also: although we are the well-beloved of Your Son, it has not yet appeared what we shall be. He looks through the lattice of our flesh, and He is fair-speaking; He has inflamed us, and we run after His fragrance. But "when He shall appear, then shall we be like Him, for we shall see Him as He is." As He is, O Lord, shall we see Him, although the time be not yet. (*Confessions* 13.15.16–18)

26

Thanks to You, O Lord. We behold the Heaven and the earth, whether the corporeal part, superior and inferior, or the spiritual and corporeal creature; and in the embellishment of these parts, of which the universal mass of the world or the universal creation consists, we see light made and divided from the darkness.

We see the firmament of Heaven, whether the primary body of the world between the spiritual upper waters and the corporeal lower waters, or — because this also is called heaven — this expanse of air, through which wander the fowls of heaven, between the waters that are in vapors borne above them, and that in clear nights drop down in dew, and those that are heavy and flow along the earth.

We behold the waters gathered together through the plains of the sea; and the dry land both void and formed, so as to be visible and compact, and the matter of herbs and trees. We behold the lights shining from above — the sun to serve the day, the moon and the stars to cheer the night; and that by all these, times should be marked and noted.

We behold on every side a humid element, fruitful with fishes, beasts, and birds; because the density of the air, which bears up the flights of birds, is increased by the exhalation of the waters.

We behold the face of the earth furnished with terrestrial creatures, and man, created after Your image and likeness, in that very image and likeness of You (that is, the power of reason and understanding) on account of which he was set over all irrational creatures.

And as in his soul there is one power that rules by directing, another made subject that it might obey, so also for the man was corporeally made a woman, who, in the mind of her rational understanding should also have a like nature, in the sex, however, of her body should be in like manner subject to the sex of her husband, as the appetite of action is subjected by reason of the mind, to conceive the skill of acting rightly. These things we behold, and they are severally good, and all very good. (*Confessions* 13.32.47)

27

O Lord God, grant Your peace unto us, for You have supplied us with all things — the peace of rest, the peace of the Sabbath, which has no evening. For all this most beautiful order of things, "very good" (all their courses being finished), is to pass away, for in them there was morning and evening. (*Confessions* 13.35.50)

28

We, therefore, see those things that You made, because they are; but they are because You see them. And we see without that they are, and within that they are good, but

You saw them there, when made, where You saw them to be made.

And we were at another time moved to do well, after our hearts had conceived of Your Spirit; but in the former time, forsaking You, we were moved to do evil; but You, the One, the Good God, have never ceased to do good.

And we also have certain good works, of Your gift, but not eternal; after these we hope to rest in Your great hallowing.

But You, being the Good, needing no good, are ever at rest, because You Yourself are Your rest. And what man will teach man to understand this? Or what angel, an angel? Or what angel, a man? Let it be asked of You, sought in You, knocked for at You; so, even so, shall it be received, so shall it be found, so shall it be opened. Amen. (*Confessions* 13.38.53)

29

"Judge me, O Lord, and separate my cause from the ungodly nation." Now, meanwhile, in this state of pilgrimage, You do not yet separate my place, because I am to live together with the "tares" even to the time of the "harvest":

You do not as yet separate my rain from theirs; my light from theirs: "separate my cause."

Let a difference be made between him who believes in You and him who does not believe in You. Our infirmity is the same; but our consciences not the same: our sufferings the same; but our longings not the same. "The desire of the ungodly shall perish," but as to the desire of the righteous, we might well doubt, if we were not sure who promised.

The object of our desires is He Himself, who promises: He will give us Himself, because He has already given Himself to us; He will give Himself in His immortality to us then immortal, even because He gave Himself in His mortality to us when mortal.

"Judge me, O God, and separate my cause from an ungodly nation: O deliver me from the deceitful and wicked man." (*Exposition on Psalm 43*, no. 2)

30

"Turn not Your face away from me." You turned it away from me when I was proud. For once I was full, and in my fullness I was puffed up. "Once in my fullness I said, I shall never be moved. I said in my fullness, I shall not be moved," knowing not Your righteousness and establishing my own; but "You, Lord, in Your will have afforded strength to my beauty."

"I said in my fullness, I shall not be moved," but from You came whatever fullness I had. And to prove to me that it was from You, "You turned Your face away from me, and I was troubled." After this trouble, into which I was cast because You turned Your face away, after the weariness of my spirit, after my heart was troubled within me because You turned Your face away, then I became "like a land without water to You": "turn not Your face away."

You turned it away from me when I was proud; give it back to me now that I am humble. "Turn not Your face away from me," because if You turn it away, "I shall be like to them that go down into the pit."

What is "that go down into the pit"? When the sinner has come into the depth of sins, he will show contempt. They "go down into the pit" who lose even confession; against which is said, "Let not the pit close her mouth over me." (*Exposition on Psalm 143*, no. 13)

31

"Be my helper: leave me not." For, behold, I am in the way, I have made the one petition of You, to dwell in Your house all the days of my life, to contemplate Your delight and be protected as Your temple: this is my one petition: but that I may attain it, I am in the way.

Perhaps You will say to me, "Strive, walk, I have given you free will; you are master of your own will, follow on the way, 'seek peace and ensue it'; turn not aside from the way, abide not therein, look not back; persevere in walking, for 'he that shall persevere to the end, the same shall be saved.'"

Now that you have received free will, you rely, as it were, on the power of walking: rely not on yourself....

"Be my helper: leave me not; neither despise me, O God of my salvation." For You who formed us help us; You who created us does not desert us. (*Second Exposition on Psalm 27*, no. 17)

32

"Hear my voice, O Lord, with which I have cried to You." Hear, Lord, my interior voice, which I have addressed to

Your ears with a strong intention. "Have mercy upon me, and hear me." Have mercy upon me, and hear me therein. (*First Exposition on Psalm 27*, no. 7)

33

"My heart has said to You, I have sought Your countenance." For I have not exhibited myself to men; but in secret, where You alone hear, my heart has said to You; I have not sought from You anything without You as a reward, but Your countenance.

"Your countenance, O Lord, will I seek." In this search will I perseveringly persist: for not anything that is common, but Your countenance, O Lord, will I seek, that I may love You freely, since nothing more precious do I find. (*First Exposition on Psalm 27*, no. 8)

34

"Turn not Your face away from me": that I may find what I seek. "Turn not aside in anger from Your servant": lest, while seeking You, I fall in with something else. For what is more grievous than this punishment to one who loves and seeks the truth of Your countenance?

"Be my helper." How shall I find it, if You help me not? "Leave me not, neither despise me, O God my Savior." Scorn not that a mortal dares to seek the Eternal; for You, God, heal the wound of my sin. (*First Exposition on Psalm 27*, no. 9)

35

O God, the true Life, of and by and in whom all things live, the common source of all good! Our faith in You excites, our hope exalts, our love unites us. . . .

I humbly beseech You, O Blessed Trinity, to come to me, to abide with me, to reign in me, to make this heart of mine a holy temple, a fit habitation for Your majesty. I entreat the Father by the Son, the Son by the Father, the Holy Spirit by the Father and the Son, that all those vicious dispositions may be removed far from me that might give offense to those eyes that cannot behold iniquity; and that all those virtues in which the God of unity delights may be implanted, and grow, and flourish, and abound in me.

O Maker and Preserver of all things visible and invisible! Keep, I beseech You, the work of Your own hands, who trusts in Your mercy alone for safety and protection. Guard me with the power of Your grace, here and in all places, now and at all times, within and without, before and behind, above and below; let Your holy angels pitch their tents around about me and so possess themselves of all the passes to my heart, so that the treacherous enemy of souls may have no place left open in which to make his approach. (*Meditations* 1.34)

36

Enable us, by the powerful influence of Your Blessed Spirit, to continue steadfast in the belief of Your truth and plentifully to bring forth the fruits agreeable to that belief; that so, by a true faith and a suitable practice, Your mercy may at last bring us to the attainment of everlasting salvation; that we may be "with You where You are," and "see You as You are," and adore the brightness of Your majesty, and join our hearts and voices with those whom You have already admitted to that glorious sight, in hymns of joy and praise. Saying with all the company of Heaven: glory to the Father, whose wisdom created us; glory to the Son, whose love redeemed us; glory to the Holy Spirit, whose graces sanctified us; glory to the almighty and undivided Trinity, whose works are inseparable, and dominion without end. To You belongs praise, and thanksgiving, and honor, and blessing: and therefore all honor, and power, and thanks, and praise be unto You our God, forever and ever. (*Meditations* 1.32)

37

Hear me, my God; hear me, light of my eyes; hear what I ask, and grant my petitions; and so that You may hear me effectually, inspire and direct my petitions. O merciful and gracious Lord! Let not my manifold offenses stop Your ears against my prayers, nor shut out Your mercy from me: but let Your servant obtain his requests, though not for any merit of his own but for the sake of His merits and intercession in whom alone he trusts and presumes by Him only to ask anything: even the Blessed Jesus, the Son of Your love, the One, the powerful "Mediator between God and man"; who, with You and Your Blessed Spirit, lives and reigns forever. Amen. (*Meditations* 1.34)

38

Sweetest, kindest, dearest Lord, most mighty King of glory, who has ascended with great triumph into Your Kingdom in Heaven and who sits enthroned at the right hand of the Father, draw me up to You; that by Your powerful guidance, and more than magnetic force, I may run after the sweet fragrance of Your ointments and not faint. Draw this thirsty soul to the rivers of eternal pleasure, to the fountain of living water, that I may drink my fill and live forever, O God of my life. (*Meditations* 1.36)

39

Pity me, O Lord, and help me according to what You see necessary for me both in body and soul. You know all things, and can do all things, and live forever, and therefore You will, I hope, consider my needs and my infirmities and extend mercy and relief in Your own time and Your own way, which is always sure to be best and most expedient for us. (*Meditations* 1.37)

40

Hear me, O Blessed Holy Trinity, and preserve me from all evil and all scandal, and especially from all deadly sin. Protect me from the subtle treachery, violent assaults, and perpetual hostilities of evil spirits, and shield me from the malice of all my enemies, visible and invisible; and under Your mighty protection, conduct me safe at last to those blissful mansions that You have prepared for those who love You, inhabited by patriarchs and prophets, apostles and martyrs, confessors and virgins, and all the holy men and women who have walked in Your fear and who have done the will of their heavenly Father faithfully from the beginning of the world. (*Meditations* 1.39)

41

Deliver me, O Lord, from the "snare of the hunter," and give not my soul up as a prey to those that seek its ruin, but keep me ever safe and steadfast in the performance of Your will. "Teach me to do the thing that pleases You, for You are my God." Give me a right judgment and a perfect understanding of divine truths so that I may have worthy apprehensions of Your unmeasurable goodness.

Direct my prayers to You on all occasions, and let me ask such things as You delight to give and are best for me to receive. (*Meditations* 1.39)

42

O Lord Jesus Christ, permit, I pray, Your unworthy servant to express his charity by enlarging these petitions, and let them prevail for blessings not only on myself but on others....

Let Your favor be ever present with Your Holy Catholic Church and with every member of it, men and women, priests and people, all who believe in You, all who labor in Your love. Increase their graces daily, and enable them faithfully to improve and persevere in every good word and work. (*Meditations* 1.39)

43

O God, the light of every heart that sees You, the life of every soul that loves You, the strength of every mind that seeks You, grant me ever to continue steadfast in Your holy love. Pour Yourself into my heart, and let it overflow and be entirely filled with Your pleasures, so that there may be no room left for the trifling vanities here below. I am ashamed and tired of living after the way of the world; the very sight and hearing of transitory objects is troublesome; help me, my God, against the insinuations of such, and be the joy of my heart: take it all to Yourself and keep Your continual residence there.

The house, I confess, is narrow; enlarge it. It is ruinous; but You repair it. It is full of pollutions that might be a nuisance to eyes so pure; I know and with grief confess it. But whose help shall I implore in cleansing it, except Yours alone?

To You, therefore, I cry instantly, begging that You will "purge me from my secret faults, and especially keep Your servant from presumptuous sins, that they never get the dominion over me."

Enable me, sweet Jesus, I beseech You, to lay aside the weight of fleshly lusts, and exchange my worldly desires and affections for those of You and Heaven. Let my body be in constant subjection to my soul, my senses to reason, and my reason to Your grace, so that both the outward and inward man may be ever obedient and disposed to do Your will. Fill my heart, my mouth, and all my bones with Your praise. Enlighten my understanding and exalt my affections, that I may soar upward to You, and set me free from those fetters that fasten me down and are an incumbrance to me, that I may leave all here below and serve, fix, and dwell upon You alone. (*Manual* 4.5)

44

I love You, O my God, and desire to love You every day more fervently. For You are beautiful and amiable above the sons of men, and You deserve an affection equal to Your own adorable and incomprehensible excellences, equal to Your marvelous instances of goodness, of which Your tender care for and unspeakable condescensions in working out the eternal salvation of mankind have given such plentiful, such astonishing proofs.

O let that fire that burns with a bright and holy flame, never languishing, never to be quenched, descend into my heart. May every part of me feel the kindly heat, may it expand itself and burn up every other passion, so that with all the dross of vain and polluted passions and desires being completely consumed, I may be turned all into love and know no other object of that love but You alone, my dearest, sweetest, and most lovely Savior....

Shine in my heart; warm, enlighten, and sanctify me, that I may be a chosen vessel for Your use: purged from all wicked filth, filled with all grace, and ever preserving all fullness. So shall I spiritually feed upon Your flesh and feel my soul effectually sustained in the strength of this heavenly banquet, so shall I be nourished unto life indeed and, living of You and ever by You, at last be conducted to You and forever rest in You.

O banquet of love, heavenly sweet, let my body be refreshed by You, my inward part overflow with the nectar of Your love, and my soul burst out with zealous expressions of Your praise continually. My God is love itself, sweeter than honey to my mouth, sustenance and joy; make me to live and grow in You. (*Manual* 4.8)

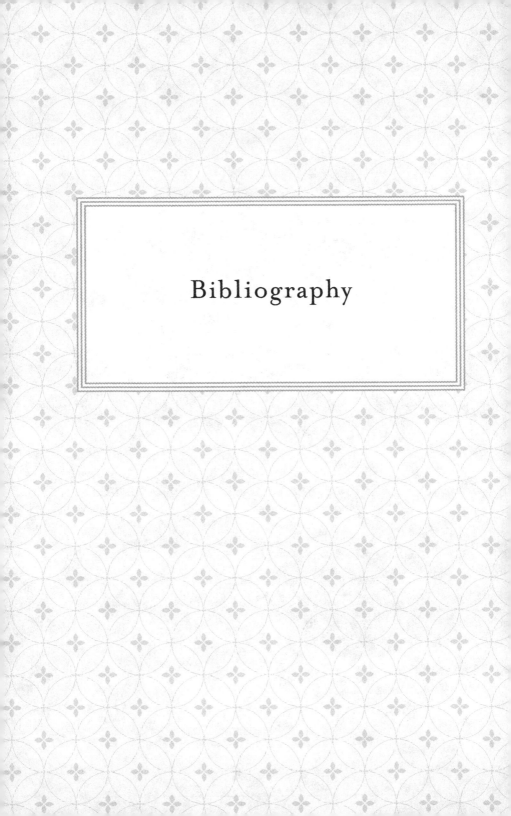

Bibliography

Augustine. *Confessions.* In *Nicene and Post-Nicene Fathers, First Series.* Vol. 1. Translated by J. G. Pilkington. Edited by Philip Schaff. Buffalo, NY: Christian Literature Publishing Co., 1887.

Augustine. *Expositions on the Book of Psalms.* 6 vols. Translated and edited by H. Walford, C. Marriott, E. B. Pusey. Oxford: John Henry Parker, 1847–1857.

Augustine. "Letter 130." In *The Letters of St. Augustine.* In *The Works of Aurelius Augustine, Bishop of Hippo.* Vol. 13. Translated by J. G. Cunningham. Edited by Marcus Dods. Edinburgh: T & T Clark, 1875.

Augustine. *Of Holy Virginity.* In *Nicene and Post-Nicene Fathers, First Series.* Vol. 3. Translated by C. L.

Cornish. Edited by Philip Schaff. Buffalo, NY: Christian Literature Publishing Co., 1887.

Augustine. *On the Trinity.* In *Nicene and Post-Nicene Fathers, First Series.* Vol. 3. Translated by Arthur West Haddan. Edited by Philip Schaff. Buffalo, NY: Christian Literature Publishing Co., 1887.

Augustine. *Sermons on the New Testament.* In *Nicene and Post-Nicene Fathers, First Series.* Vol. 6. Translated by R. G. MacMullen. Edited by Philip Schaff. Buffalo, NY: Christian Literature Publishing Co., 1888.

Augustine. *Tractates on the Gospel of John.* In *Nicene and Post-Nicene Fathers, First Series.* Vol. 7. Translated by John Gibb. Edited by Philip Schaff. Buffalo, NY: Christian Literature Publishing Co., 1888.

The Meditations of St. Augustine: His Treatise of the Love of God, Soliloquies, and Manual. Translated by George Stanhope. London: Printed for J. Nunn et al., 1818.

Schaff, Philip, ed. *The Early Church Fathers and Other Works. Translated by R. G. Macmullen.* Edinburgh: William B. Eerdmans, 1867.

Sermon 206, no. 3; *Sermon 123*, no. 5; *Sermon 216*, no. 7; *Sermon 265*, no. 10; *The Free Choice of the Will* 2.16.43; *Sermon 188*, no. 2; *Sermon 184*, no. 3; *Sermon 203*, no. 3; *Sermon 262*, no. 4; *Sermon 262*, nos. 5–6; *Sermon 196*, no. 3; *Sermon 261*, no. 1; *Sermon 261*, no. 9; *The Christian Combat* 11; *Sermon 333*, no. 7; *Sermon 211*, no. 5; *Sermon 132*, no. 4; *Sermon 225*, no. 4; *Sermon 67*, no. 10; and parts of *Confessions* 4.10.15. Translated by Laura Bement. March 2023.

The Soliloquies of St. Augustine. Translated by Rose Elizabeth Cleveland. Boston: Little, Brown, and Co., 1910.

About the Author

SARA PARK McLAUGHLIN, author of four nonfiction books, taught freshman English at Texas Tech University for thirty-four years. Her book *Meeting God in Silence* (Tyndale 1993) was later translated into Korean and published in Seoul (Word of Life, 2000). She is a former award-winning newspaper columnist for the *Lubbock Avalanche Journal* and the *Amarillo Globe-News* and has published numerous scholarly articles about C. S. Lewis, G. K. Chesterton, and her original theory of humor. Now retired and living in Wisconsin, she is enjoying writing a series entitled "Misunderstanding Catholicism" for her blog: www.medium.com/@sara.mclaughlin.

Sophia Institute

Sophia Institute is a nonprofit institution that seeks to nurture the spiritual, moral, and cultural life of souls and to spread the gospel of Christ in conformity with the authentic teachings of the Roman Catholic Church.

Sophia Institute Press fulfills this mission by offering translations, reprints, and new publications that afford readers a rich source of the enduring wisdom of mankind.

Sophia Institute also operates the popular online Catholic resource CatholicExchange.com. *Catholic Exchange* provides world news from a Catholic perspective as well as daily devotionals and articles that will help readers to grow in holiness and live a life consistent with the teachings of the Church.

In 2013, Sophia Institute launched Sophia Institute for Teachers to renew and rebuild Catholic culture through service to Catholic education. With the goal of nurturing the spiritual, moral, and cultural life of souls, and an abiding respect for the role and work of teachers, we strive to provide materials and programs that are at once enlightening to the mind and ennobling to the heart; faithful and complete, as well as useful and practical.

Sophia Institute gratefully recognizes the Solidarity Association for preserving and encouraging the growth of our apostolate over the course of many years. Without their generous and timely support, this book would not be in your hands.

www.SophiaInstitute.com
www.CatholicExchange.com
www.SophiaInstituteforTeachers.org

Sophia Institute Press® is a registered trademark of Sophia Institute.
Sophia Institute is a tax-exempt institution as defined by the
Internal Revenue Code, Section 501(c)(3). Tax ID 22-2548708.